The Historical Romance

Popular Fictions Series
Series editors:
Tony Bennett
Associate Professor, School of Humanities, Griffith University
Graham Martin
Professor of English Literature, Open University

In the same series

Cover stories
Narrative and ideology in the British spy thriller
Michael Denning
Combining cultural history with narrative analysis, Michael Denning
tracks the spy thriller from John Buchan to Eric Ambler, Ian
Fleming and John Le Carré, and shows how these tales tell a history
of our times, and attempt to resolve crises and contradictions in
ideologies of nation and empire, of class and gender.

Lost Narratives
Popular fictions, politics and recent history
Roger Bromley
Explores the ways in which certain popular cultural forms – narrative
fictions, autobiographical writings, television productions –
contribute to the social production of memory.

Popular Film and Television Comedy
Steve Neale and Frank Krutnik
Explores the nature of comedy, relating its diverse forms and
conventions to their institutional contexts. The authors discuss a
wide range of programmes and films, looking in particular detail at
slapstick and 'screwball' comedies and TV programmes such as
Monty Python, Hancock and *Steptoe and Son.*

Popular Fiction
Technology, Ideology, Production, Reading
Edited by Tony Bennett
Brings together key essays on literary, filmic and televisual forms of
popular fiction, introducing the main genres of popular fiction, from
science fiction to the Western, 'film noir' to comedy, and in so doing
outlines the debates and cultural questions which their analysis
raises. A central text for students of media, literature, and cultural
studies.

The Historical Romance

Helen Hughes

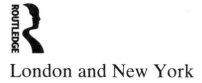

London and New York

First published 1993
by Routledge
11 New Fetter Lane, London EC4P 4EE

Simultaneously published in the USA and Canada
by Routledge
29 West 35th Street, New York, NY 10001

Typeset in 10 on 12 point Times by
Computerset, Harmondsworth, Middlesex
Printed in Great Britain by Biddles Ltd, Guildford and King's Lynn

British Library Cataloguing in Publication Data
A catalogue record for this book is available from the British Library

Library of Congress Cataloging in Publication Data
Hughes, Helen
 The historical romance/Helen Hughes.
  p. cm. — (Popular fictions series)
 Includes bibliographical references.
  1. English fiction—20th century—History and criticism. 2. Historical
fiction, English—History and criticism. 3. Love stories, English—History
and criticism. I. Title. II. Series: Popular fiction series.
PR888.H5H84   1993
823'.08109'0904—dc20   92-2456

ISBN 0–415–05812–0

Contents

Series editors' preface

There are many good reasons for studying popular fiction. The best, though, is that it matters. In the many and varied forms in which they are produced and circulated – by the cinema, broadcasting institutions and the publishing industry – popular fictions saturate the rhythms of everyday life. In doing so, they help to define our sense of our selves, shaping our desires, fantasies, imagined pasts and projected futures. An understanding of such fictions – of how they are produced and circulated, organized and received – is thus central to an understanding of our selves; of how these selves have been shaped and of how they might be changed.

This series is intended to contribute to such an understanding by providing a context in which different traditions and directions in the study of popular fiction might be brought into contact so as to interanimate one another. It will thus range across the institutions of cinema, broadcasting and publishing, seeking to illuminate both their respective specificities as well as the relations between them with a view to identifying the ways in which popular film, television and writing interact as parts of developed cultural technologies for the formation of subjectivities. Consideration of the generic properties of popular fiction will thus be situated within an analysis of their historical and institutional conditions of production and reception.

Similarly, the series will represent, and co-ordinate a debate between, the diverse political perspectives through which the study of popular fiction has been shaped and defined in recent years. Feminist studies of the part popular fictions play in the production of gendered subjectivities and relations; Marxist perspectives on the relations between popular fictions and class formations; popular fiction as a site for the reproduction and contestation of subordinate racial and national identities: in encompassing contributions from these often sharply contrasting traditions of thought the series will explore the complex and intertwining web of political relations in which the production and reception of popular fictions are involved.

It should be clear, though, that in all this our aim is not to transform popular fiction into something else – into literature, say, or art cinema. If the study of popular fiction matters it is because what is ultimately at stake in such analysis is the production of a better popular fiction as well as of better, politically more productive ways of reading it.

Tony Bennett
Graham Martin

Acknowledgements

The material which formed the basis of this book was originally presented in the form of a thesis for the Doctor of Philosophy degree at the University of Bradford. To Ken Smith, my supervisor, I am particularly grateful for support, ideas and guidance. I am grateful also to Kathie Jowett for her expert typing of the manuscript. Graham Martin and Tony Bennett both read the manuscript and offered invaluable advice and encouragement. Lastly, I owe thanks to my husband for his patience and support throughout the gestation of this book.

Chapter 1

Introduction

In describing modern romantic novels as a 'lax sort of romance'[1] Gillian Beer called attention to two important qualities of the genre: an element of fantasy, distancing the story from the everyday world of the reader, and the popular nature of the genre – 'lax' suggesting a denigratory tone as well as the combination of verisimilitude and fantasy which gives such texts their 'realism'.

These are significant qualities. 'Realism' allows the text to be consumed as surrogate experience, while fantasy gives an opportunity for wish-fulfilling motifs which symbolically represent the hopes and fears of the readership. The setting of historical romance provides just that necessary mingling of 'distance' and 'reality' which allows this to happen. The 'past' presented may be as imaginary as the forests of medieval romance, the detail selectively chosen and the interpretation subjective, but an impression of an accurate representation of a past reality, which led to the contemporary world of the reader through a sequence of cause and effect, is given by the use of period detail and reference to familiar historical issues.

Such representation is both convincing and estranging. The artificially constructed 'past' is presented as 'what really happened', but it is also a suitably exotic context for the romantic motifs which reflect – sometimes by contraries – the concerns of the readers. Historical romance thus provides a useful subject for the study of the ways in which an artificial 'past' can gain 'mythical' significance, confirming attitudes or highlighting fears and hopes which arise from the nature of contemporary society. This study is the aim of the present book.

*

In the early years of this century, my father used to read the books of Stanley Weyman, his sister reading over his shoulder. My brother used to lend me Rafael Sabatini's cloak-and-dagger romances after he had read them. Much later, college friends gave me books by Georgette Heyer to read, as though this was some kind of female rite of passage. There seemed to be little in common between the experiences. Yet, on reflection, the books were more alike than might appear at first sight.

Nothing could be further from the clash of swords, swift chases on horseback and secret plots of the earlier romances than the social comedy of Heyer's Regency love-stories. Yet, though the atmosphere was different, the stories themselves had an uncanny similarity. Told without circumstantial detail, the individual situations – even, in some cases, the complete plots – were the same. Their links with each other were closer than with other novels – contemporary adventure or love stories – and they seemed to form a species of their own. It was one which was characterized by distinctive stock situations and stereotyped characters. The books could be differentiated from historical fiction as a whole by their formulaic and fantastic character.

Although the term 'historical romance' is sometimes used indiscriminately by publishers and booksellers for historical novels of all descriptions, the name is more commonly reserved for books of this type. It is, in fact, a very suitable one, since one characteristic which all these novels have in common is a romantic story.

Gillian Beer, writing of romance in the 'Critical Idiom' series, lists some eight or nine features by which this genre is characterized. 'Romance', she says, 'invokes the past or the socially remote', and tends to be set in 'an aristocratic and idealized world'.[2] This distant setting is, however, realized in great detail, and emotional reactions and relationships are presented with a fullness which gives an impression of verisimilitude, despite the unlikelihood of much of the action. The major themes of romance are adventure and sexual love, with a narrow range of behaviour and experience being portrayed. Well-known stories, reassuring in their familiarity, are used and re-used. For essentially the romance is written to entertain: it frees the reader from 'inhibitions and preoccupations' by drawing him or her into its own world.

All romantic historical fiction contains a good many common features. Setting is subordinate to plot. The social world portrayed is primarily an aristocratic one. In fact, the characteristics of the books conform well enough to Gillian Beer's list of the characteristics of romance to justify their grouping under the general title of 'historical romance'.

It is the nature of its stock situations which links historical 'cloak-and-dagger' fiction most clearly to romance. Abductions, escapes, rescues, disguises and unknown identities have been the mainstay of romantic plots since the days of the first Greek romances by Longinus, Achilles Tatius and their fellows. Margaret Williamson has suggested that the situations are older: the stories of the early Greek romances, Williamson suggests, originated in 'widespread traditional story material'.[3] The basic material of romance was thus 'already ancient' when the first ones were written.

At the same time, for all that the books share, there is clearly a difference between the novels of Weyman and the novels of Heyer; a difference which is also to be found between the books of their respective followers. Whereas the novels of Stanley Weyman (1855–1928), Rafael Sabatini (1875–1950) and their contemporaries (such as 'Henry Seton Merriman' – Hugh Stowell Scott (1862–1903) – A. E. W. Mason (1865 – 1948), or Sir Arthur Conan Doyle (1858–1930) could be read with equal enjoyment by both sexes, the romances of Georgette Heyer (1904–74), as her biographer Jane Aiken Hodge has noted, were written 'mainly for women'.[4] The adventurous, cloak-and-dagger yarns of the former dominated the market in the early part of the century; Heyer's own early work was in fact of this type. After the early 1930s, however, the swashbuckling yarn seems to have lost its appeal; a few writers, like Sabatini, continued to write the same kind of book and find a market until the 1950s, but their work was beginning to seem decidedly old-fashioned. After this decade, historical romance became predominantly a woman's genre, which it had certainly never been before.

This in itself was an interesting development. What was, perhaps, of greatest significance about the change, however, was that in so many ways there was no change; the later stories for women were so similar in plot and characterization to the earlier adventure stories that a continuous line of development could be traced from the beginning of the century to the 1980s. In nearly a hundred years the genre has been remarkably conservative. Yet one audience had been lost, another won. Does this mean that the situations of historical romance had a particular significance for its readers, one which could change as their circumstances changed? The answer must lie in examining the uses to which both the situations of romance and the setting in the past were put.

Umberto Eco, writing of *The Name of the Rose* in *Encounter*,[5] distinguished three kinds of writing about the past: fantasy, swashbuckling romance, and novels which give a strong feeling of a specific time and place. Of these, the two last both give at least an impression of using an authentic historical background. Thus swashbuckling 'romance' contains real historical figures in central roles. In 'Dreaming of the Middle Ages', Eco again refers to the importance of authentic historical figures in supporting the credibility of the fictions of 'cloak-and-dagger' fiction ('think of Dumas and the crucial narrative role played by such characters as Richelieu and Louis XIII'),[6] adding that the fictional characters themselves are not especially characteristic of their place and time. In such novels the 'past' setting is a 'pretext' which 'helps one to enjoy the fictional characters'. In historical novels proper, however, the characters may be fictional, but they 'tell us something "true"'[7] about their period because they are representative of it. The aim of such novels is to gain a better understanding, not only of the period chosen, but also of the present as an 'end result of those remote historical events'.[8]

That 'cloak-and-dagger' romances use the past as a colourful background of the kind described by Eco as 'pretext' is clear enough from a glance at some of the texts described in this book, such as those by Weyman or Sabatini, where details of the past which seem exotic or quaint are often foregrounded to give a flavour of the period setting. I would argue, however, that Eco's taxonomy, though very useful in drawing attention to differences in function, is too limiting; the use of the past as pretext, and the use of the 'remote historical events' of the novel as precursors of the present are not mutually exclusive. This is especially true of Conan Doyle and Weyman, but it is true to some extent of other cloak-and-dagger writers as well, such as Orczy and Sabatini.

The past setting may in such texts appear to add to the pleasure of the book because it can be presented as more colourful and exciting that the everyday life of the reader; but it may also be seen as the amniotic fluid in which the seeds of the present float. Tendencies can be isolated in a historic period, which, however alien that time may seem, none the less prefigure characteristics of the contemporary world.

Eco's function of the past as 'pretext' is to be found more exclusively in the 'Regencies': the works of Heyer and her followers.

In these books the past setting is attractive because it is different, a holiday from reality. As Janice Radway has written of reading such books, the experience 'will be marked not as "work" but as "pleasure"',[9] and the pleasure derives in large part from entering a novel and glamorous world. Even so, there is relevance to the present in these novels too: the picture of the past is attractive because of attitudes in the reader which derive from experience in the present, and which are confirmed by reading the texts.

Harry Henderson has pointed out, in his account of historical fiction, *Versions of the Past*,[10] that a historical novel functions as an 'inverted utopia': a whole past society has to be recreated, and because of its unfamiliarity the structure is necessarily laid bare. It is not, however, a positivistic assemblage of facts about the past, but 'an imaginative ordering of materials in an attempt at the recreation of experience'.

None the less it can be said that there are differences of effect, even within the genre of historical romance, and that the author's materials are ordered according to his or her view of the function of history. Romantic writers use the past as an exotic setting to add to the 'escape' value of their stories; but it also functions as a mirror for the present. Partly because of their very difference from that of the reader's familiar world, forms of past society can be represented as ideal in some of their aspects without losing their verisimilitude. Equally, features of present-day society may be presented for criticism if they are shown, appropriately modified (in embryo, perhaps), embedded in a historical context. The effect is to defamiliarize them, encouraging a stricter scrutiny.

This is true to some extent of all the texts covered by this book, but it is the most striking aspect of the work of some of the novelists, such as Weyman. For other writers, the circumstances of a past society produce what is virtually a different kind of human nature, so that historical periods are seen as self-sufficient with no overt link to the present. This more holistic approach has usually been favoured by writers in the tradition of Scott – Conan Doyle is the most obvious example among the texts covered here – whose aim is to enable the reader to reconstruct the past as accurately as possible.

It is an aim which derives from a view of history which would scarcely have been recognizable before the nineteenth century. Raymond Chapman has remarked on the Victorian sense of 'modernity', an awareness of the age as different from the past,[11] and Avrom Fleishman has noted an interest in historicity which derived in part from the Romantic movement and in part from a feeling that industrialization had cut contemporary society cleanly from the older world.[12] Stephen Bann has linked historical fiction – and, indeed, other 'texts' or forms of organized discourse as well, ranging from museums to the architectural environment of poets – to a new attitude towards historiography. The early nineteenth century saw the development of a 'concern for cognitive values', exemplified in the work of Leopold von Ranke; at the same time, 'historians, poets, novelists, collectors . . . are experiencing the elation of a new and concrete vision of the past'.[13] The two views were linked, the stringently scrutinized facts and concepts of one approach providing the skeletal base on which the reconstructions of the other were built – though the 'hardness' of the facts does not in such cases guarantee the kind of neutrality which many of the texts appear to claim.

On the other hand, the holistic approach is followed by the more escapist of the romancers. Such writers are concerned above all to suggest what Scott, in the preface to *Waverley*, called 'the remote picturesqueness'[14] of a setting in the past – an aim which does not preclude the highlighting of carefully placed details attesting to the depth of the author's historical research.

Such authors differ from the 'reconstructers', too, in that their books are predicated upon the assumption that human nature remains essentially the same in all times and all places. The idea that a historical novel provides an opportunity for the study of permanent human characteristics (what Scott, in the preface to *Waverley*, called 'those passions common to men in all stages of society'[15] underlies to some degree all the romances studied in this book. While it helps to explain the sense of relevance they invoke, it is based on the notion of an indissoluble core to the individual human personality which is essentially Romantic and bourgeois, and which marginalizes the role of socialization and culture. The very realism of the narrative form, for all its fantastic content, naturalizes such assumptions, since it is a mode familiar from the Victorian novel in which such a unitary view of the personality was strongly promoted.

Moreover, the idea of permanent human characteristics make plausible the notion that some features of society can also be shown as existing at all times and so, by implication, as 'natural' – change being thus impossible and attempts to produce it perhaps harmful.

None the less, since the past is different from the present, it may well contain features which are disturbing or obnoxious. It is possible that such features may simply be edited out of the historical setting: a 'sanitizing' of the past of which most romancers are to some extent guilty. In any case, however, the past setting makes such features' safe' for the reader because it is 'closed off', 'finished'. Even if the societies of the past show tendencies which have come to full development in the present, less tolerable features can be taken as having withered in the process of historical change which developed the more desirable aspects. There is no need for the author to make this explicit: the very fact that the reader can deplore some aspects of the past shows a change of attitude.

The romances studied in this book have all taken advantage to some extent of both these features of historical fiction, to touch upon aspects of society which may have been seen as problematic in the author's day and to present an implied resolution, not so much by confronting what is problematic as by sealing the problem in the past or by showing it as leading to a present good – often, by using both methods.

An illuminating commentary can be found in the work of two recent writers. For Harry Henderson, the recreation of the past in fiction partakes of the nature of 'myth', in line with Lévi-Strauss's definition of the term: history is both 'a sequence of past happenings' and 'a timeless pattern' which can be seen in the structures of contemporary social experience and helps us to understand it better.[16] Claud Cockburn used the term in a slightly different sense in *Bestseller*:[17] a picture of a past society which functions as myth is unreal, but appeals to and expresses the deep-seated, inarticulate concerns of its readers.

These two senses, however, are not incompatible. Cockburn's inarticulate concerns are about the nature of contemporary events and, since history is a *social* science, of contemporary society. Lévi-Strauss's 'timeless pattern' is one which gives an overt structure to our perceptions of contemporary society; and Cockburn's unreal picture of the past, in addressing the reader's concerns, produces just such a structure. Even if the myth created seems to offer little more than wish-fulfilment, those wishes arise from perceptions which are far from being 'merely' escapist. An escape, as Cockburn points out, must be *from* something and *to* something, and the starting point determines the ultimate point of arrival. An 'escapist' fiction is still an inverted utopia, conditioned by perceptions of the society which gave it birth and in which it is received.

Nor is the past presented by 'serious' fiction necessarily any less 'unreal' than that in 'escapist' texts. The notion of a 'real' past which can in some way be captured undistorted in a historical text is itself a product of history. At the end of the nineteenth century, Lord Acton, as Stephen Bann has pointed out, praised Leopold von Ranke for his 'colourless, critical writing';[18] a style which, he believed, had 'transparency to the facts'. Such a comment presupposes the unproblematically truthful and complete nature of a reality which lies behind the text: a reality to which the text gives access. This uncritical acceptance of 'historical reality' suggests the validity, in relation to historical romance, of a third definition of myth: that of Roland Barthes, who defines 'myth' as a semiological system which gives a 'natural' image of a 'reality' that has actually been fabricated within a historical past.[19] Even an account of historical 'reality' which seems neutral is actually – through selection of 'facts' or their interpretation – an ideologically charged construction.

Historical novels, based on a version of history and to some extent validated by it, are permeated by the ideology of the version of the past they present; but it is the history which seems the 'true' element of the narrative, and thus the least politicized aspect of the text. This account of historical romance assumes, however, that the presentation of history is as much a part of the 'myth of the past' as the invented story.

*

In the historical romances written between 1890 and 1990 which are the subject of this book, a move from presenting the past as progenitor of the present to presenting it as self-enclosed and different from the present can be detected. Sir Arthur Conan Doyle, Stanley Weyman, and, to a lesser extent, Rafael Sabatini, show history as a process of change, leading towards a present which, seen in the light of these historical processes, may be viewed favourably.

The appeal of a writer such as Jeffrey Farnol or Georgette Heyer is different, however. A sense of a development towards the present is irrelevant in reading their books: they create a self-sufficient past world whose attractions are seductive, drawing the reader into an uncritical experience of history as real life. The ingredients of this world may be familiar everyday events but they are heightened and sanitized by the imagination. None the less, they do have a base in the real world, in being an expression of real hopes and fears. When what that base is and how it has been modified are seen, the messages of the text – which thus concern the contemporary world of author and reader – can be understood.

The writers whose works provide a central focus for this study have been chosen because in their heyday they sold widely, and because they wrote a particular kind of historical romance: one which sets imaginary characters among real past incidents, with real historical figures appearing on the periphery rather than in the centre of the action.

Although these limits exclude a number of very popular writers, this kind of novel allows a freer play to the imagination and so provides a clearer reflection of the attitudes and perceptions which lie behind the story. In addition, the texts chosen exemplify some of the more interesting developments which took place during the period from the end of the nineteenth century to the present: the period during which the form of popular historical romance changed so markedly.

Typical historical stories of the 1890s are about dangerous adventures, usually in an open-air setting, and set in a context of some crucial point of historical change. Sir Arthur Conan Doyle, whose *The White Company* dates from 1891, is the writer whose reputation has endured the longest, perhaps fortuitously, since his historical romances, though popular, were not the most widely read of their kind. The fame of Sherlock Holmes, however, has ensured their survival, and they continue to be read, particularly by young people. These certainly conform to the 'open-air adventure' type. The dominant writer of this kind of romance at the turn of the century, however, was Stanley Weyman. His books are almost forgotten now, but his great contemporary popularity makes his work a particularly interesting study. Books by one of the most popular of his contemporaries, A. E. W. Mason, are considered as well.

In the early years of the twentieth century a younger generation of writers was responsible for a number of significant developments in the genre which went some way towards preparing for the more radical change that took place in the 1920s. Some of the most popular and interesting of these include Rafael Sabatini, Baroness Orczy (1865 – 1947), whose reputation rests largely upon her creation of the Scarlet Pimpernel, and Jeffrey Farnol (1878 – 1952), whose best-selling romance *The Broad Highway*, published in 1910, was noted by Claud Cockburn[20] as a new development in historical fiction. Farnol may be seen as moving away from even the partial realism of Weyman to the creation of a full-blown fantasy world, though in other ways his adventurous stories were more like those of Weyman than those of Sabatini and Orczy were.

These writers continued to write as late as the 1950s; their books remain on the library shelves, but they became increasingly thought of as books for young people. This may be seen in their appearance on the lists of retailers specializing in children's books, such as 'Books for Students'; and, in an article in *The Times Literary Supplement* of 21 September 1984[21] Gillian Avery remembered the historical adventure story as something she had enjoyed in her own childhood. She considered it now to be a thing of the past, its place having been taken by the historical love-story which is particularly associated with the name of Georgette Heyer.

Heyer's work can be seen as marking a point of transition: when she began to write in the early 1920s she produced 'cloak-and-dagger' romances of the type popularized by Sabatini and Orczy. Before the end of the decade she had developed a new kind of romance, relying much more on social comedy and centering on a love-story rather than upon adventure. It proved a popular combination; her books became best-sellers, just as Weyman's or Farnol's had been in their day, but with a predominantly female readership.

Her popularity ensured that she had successors: some, hailed as new Heyers by the publishers, imitated her closely, while others, such as Barbara Cartland, largely dropped the comic element to give more prominence to the love-story.

During the decades from the 1930s to the 1960s – a period roughly contemporary with Heyer's own career – her kind of historical romance remained the dominant form of historical fiction. Such books were marketed as women's romances; Heyer's own first publishers were the firm whose name has become almost synonymous with the genre, Mills & Boon. Although they are still published, it is rare now to find this kind of novel in the best-seller lists. Other variants of historical fiction became popular in their turn: the 'bodice-ripper' of the 1970s, for instance, or the sagas of the 1980s. To examine the relationship between these and the social and economic attitudes of the time would in itself be a rewarding study, but, although they retain many features in common with the romances, the line of development is not so clear. Hence, this enquiry is confined to the more traditional romance, while noting the existence of other kinds.

Women's historical romance has never been over-concerned with presenting a picture of the past as a time of historical change; like Farnol, authors of women's fiction have tried to create a seductive past world whose chief attraction is its essential difference from the present. But their treatment of one aspect of life provides an exception to this: that concerned with the relationship between the sexes and the role of women in society.

Writers of adventure stories such as Weyman and Sabatini were interested in these, too, but their concerns were more wide-ranging, since their stories derive their tension from some impending danger to the state or to society. Hence, the setting is often a time of revolution or of war. Their picture of past society thus necessarily includes a number of opposed groups, national, religious or social.

A writer whose intention is to provide a serious commentary on history, such as Conan Doyle, presents incidents which imply some kind of social critique – of the period which forms the story's setting, and, by implication, of the writer's own contemporary world. Traces of some such critique can be found even in the work of the less 'serious' writers whose books are more typical of the genre. Essentially, such traces occur in the areas noted above: the picture presented of relationships between the sexes and their social roles, the image of a national identity, and the relationships between social classes which may be extended to include a general image of political activity. The analysis of attitudes consciously presented by each author examined here will consequently focus on these areas.

In addition, however, each writer gives unconscious evidence of attitudes which, since they arise from the very nature of their own society, are so taken for granted that they seem to be the natural way of things and not a socially constructed picture of the world. Such attitudes become evident through noting the contradictions and omissions in the image of the world presented by the story.

Historical romance provides a particularly fertile field for such an examination, because of its dual nature. On the one hand, it provides a conscious critique of society through the presentation of a past world. On the other, however, it strings together a number of romantic incidents whose popularity arises more from their mythic quality than any pretensions they may have to realism. The attitudes suggested by such incidents frequently undermine those which the writer seems most anxious to promote.

The significant items among this stock of romantic characters and incidents will be described in more detail in the following chapter. In general, however, they are familiar enough: who does not recognize the saturnine, often brutal hero of women's romance, the spirited heroine who challenges him and succumbs to his *force majeure*, or the abductions and escapes typical of the romantic genres? They can be found in historical romances of the nineteenth as well as the twentieth century; historical romance of the traditional kind gives them a vehicle for survival even today. What originality the individual books have is given by the setting, the historical events which form the starting point for the story, and specific details of character and situation. Such a mode of construction has an effect on the way in which the reader approaches the book, a point which will be considered in more detail later.

While the consciously presented themes of the novels relate clearly to political and social attitudes current at the time they were written, the relationships of the stock characters and situations of the romantic story are less obvious. None the less, links do exist, arising from the 'mythic' nature of the situations. These embody – sometimes to challenge, more often to confirm – many of the most important power relationships of the society in which the stories had their origin and, to a lesser extent, of those in which they remain widely read.

It is this characteristic, one that historical romances have in common with other forms of popular fiction, which makes a genre whose constituents have in general few claims to literary merit a worthwhile object of enquiry. 'Popular-culture texts', as Graham Martin has written,[22] offer 'symbolic means of identification with, and symbolic means of dissent from, the society in which we live.' One of the purposes of the present study, therefore, is to consider the ways in which popular historical writers use both the past, and the romantic situations for which it provides a suitable setting, as a symbol for the kind of identification and dissent to which Martin refers.

Chapter 2

The structures of historical romance

Historical romance, with its links with both 'history'and the novel, is a genre in which two systems of myth operate: the archetypal episodes of romance, which in themselves are part of the semiological system described by Barthes in *Mythologies*,[1] and the presentation of history. These systems operate concurrently, one sometimes supporting and confirming, sometimes undermining, the messages of the other. The reader is not necessarily aware of such contradictions, however, because to receive the message of the text she or he has to 'read' its structures, and these enable a variety of information to be carried without unduly exposing any inconsistency. In this chapter, the ways in which the structures of historical romance allow this to happen will be explored.

The writing of one of the best-known of historical romancers, Barbara Cartland, has been characterized by Rosalind Brunt[2] as a process of '*bricolage*' or 'do-it-yourself'; the phrase implying, presumably, the putting together of items from a stock kit to create a product which as a whole has a certain individuality but consists of standard parts. The term, originally Lévi-Strauss's, was applied by him to the myths of primitive societies, but Brunt's account shows how applicable it is to popular literature, and to historical romance in particular.

To continue the analogy, the basic kit units which are used to make up the plots of historical romance are stock situations and character-types which can be found in book after book, rearranged or redeployed, demonstrating minor differences of detail but with an essential structural identity.

This, of course, is to say that the genre is as dependent on formulae as other popular fiction is. The stock situations form part of the repertoire which the reader brings to each individual text, once familiar with the genre. They ease the task of reading, since their appearance in the text is easy to recognize; the reader can orientate him- or herself quickly, and is able to bring anticipation into play. Because the detail of each plot is different, there is no sense of reading a story whose outcome is already known, rather of becoming aware of a series of options, some pleasant, some not, which are gradually reduced until the outcome is revealed.

The motifs have evolved because the options they embody offer peculiar satisfactions. Calamitous or triumphal, they realize in symbolic form the hopes and fears of the readers. The avoidance of particular kinds of failure is as important as the happy outcome: suspense comes because the threatened failure somehow touches a nerve in the reader's consciousness.

Historical romance has its particular stock of such motifs. To some extent, the stock has changed since the end of the last century. Adventure stories of the 1890s and early 1900s characteristically centred around a mission whose outcome was of public significance. Such plots could be slotted into known historical contexts – the French Revolution of *The Scarlet Pimpernel* (1905), for example, or the French Wars of Religion which provided a setting for many of Stanley Weyman's adventure stories. The familiar historical settings were themselves a sign of the derivative character of these stories; there were continual echoes of older authors, such as Alexandre Dumas in the case of Weyman's books, or Dickens in the case of Orczy's. The very structure of the stories, which made such events a setting for an imaginary adventure, was in the tradition of Scott or G. P. R. James.

The sphere of public activity was foregrounded in these stories, and the interests of the hero were predominant. The books re-affirmed the nature of society as rewarding public action with success. Social stability and, dependent upon it, individual happiness were seen as arising from political and military activity, which, consequently, was presented as prestigious and valuable. These activities were initiated and carried through almost entirely by men; women's function was presented as subordinate. They could act, in Propp's terms,[3] as helper, or, more rarely, as sender; in the work of some authors, notably A. E. W. Mason, they can be a positive hindrance to action.

Masculine activity, seen as being characteristically in the public sphere, was, therefore, the main fount of positive values in the text. The source of these, however, was further limited since the hero of these romances was at least a gentleman, and probably an aristo-crat. This was faithful to the nature of romance, but carried with it the impression that political activity was an exclusively upper-class concern, the prerogative of the 'natural leaders' of society – an impression reinforced by the unfavourable presentation of those upsurges of popular unrest which were often one element in the hero's situation.

This might seem to exclude the very readers to whom the books made their greatest appeal. The excluding cues were to some extent counteracted, however, by other situations, connected with the 'love' element of the romance. These were perhaps more relevant to the concerns of the average reader, giving him or her a location in the text. The disguises and concealments arising from the hero's mission, the subsequent misunderstandings, conflicts and recon-ciliations between heroes and heroines, the rescues which reveal that a hero cares for the heroine after all: all these are situations which make up the detail of the plot in book after book.

In the outcome of these situations, the union of hero and heroine is as important as the success of the mission. The incidents are thus related to activities in the private sphere, and the values they imply are embodied in the heroine rather than in the hero. The heroine, all but useless in an adventure, is none the less important as a carer (an injury to the hero, to be tended by the heroine, is a strikingly frequent motif); the domestic qualities she represents may be defended by the hero, but they are also ones which he has to learn to share.

The heroes of 'adventure' romances are strong in the qualities demanded by public activity – they are courageous, ingenious in strategy, and good at commanding men – but they need to learn how to cope with the women characters. In doing so, they take upon themselves some of the characteristics of the heroine – sensitivity to the needs of others and gentleness, for instance. Union with the heroine often means withdrawing with her into a domestic life where such values hold sway. A thematic conflict is thus set up, the nature of which I will explore in more detail in later chapters. The overall effect, however, is to reinforce a view of society as centred around a particular image of the family, a society made safe by the government of its natural leaders – that is, men of upper- or upper-middle-class origin.

The conflicts, disguises, abductions and rescues which, though linked with the public 'mission', belong to the private sphere, are the traditional motifs of romance mentioned in Chapter 1. Their ancient origin suggests an appeal which can be adapted to a wide variety of changing circumstances. This is presumably because their significance, which is concerned primarily with the individual and his or her relationship with society, remains stable even when times change.

Of all these situations, the 'disguise' motif is perhaps the most frequent and important. It implies a change of social status, and the concealment of the character's true personality and motivation. This is turn suggests a particular view of human nature as having an unchanging unified core beneath surface appearances. The nature of the individual is strongly linked with his or her social status, and the stress on the revelation of the true attributes of a personality suggests the importance attached to it.

According to this view, society may be seen as essentially individualistic, with self-fulfilment the chief end of all activity. The ideal society is one which promotes this, even when such a society promotes the interests of the strongest and most gifted. Implicit in these motifs, therefore, is an acceptance – even a celebration – of the unequal distribution of wealth and power as offering a means of rewarding the deserving and those entitled to a large share of them by nature.

As, during the course of the twentieth century, the 'public' element of adventurous missions began to wither away, plots based on status, disguise, and individual conflict or reconciliation took their place. In books such as Sabatini's *The Tavern Knight* of 1904, private revenge for loss of status was much more important than the hero's role in the Civil War which provided a context for the story. The adventure element never died away completely. The plot of Barbara Cartland's 1974 romance *The Bored Bridegroom*, for instance, is strikingly like that of Orczy's *The Scarlet Pimpernel* of 1905, with a hero whose mission is to save aristocrats from the guillotine. The story had presumably retained its appeal, but the focus had changed, none the less. In the later romance what is important is not the adventure but the opportunity it offers for the reconciliation of the estranged bride and the bridegroom of the title.

Although the stories of Farnol and Sabatini, whose plots reduced the importance of public missions to focus on private quests and conflicts, appealed widely between 1910 and the late 1920s, the location of positive values in the heroine meant that these plots were really more suited to female-centred romance.

In the books of Georgette Heyer, Barbara Cartland and their followers, the actual situations remain the same as in the earlier books, but the centrality of the heroine's concerns has led to a shift of emphasis. The conflict between hero and heroine, the tending of the hero and the rescue of the heroine, and the other motifs familiar from the adventure romance, take their place as part of a consideration of female destiny, power relationships between men and women, and the function of marriage. Details of social activity (such as the balls and fashions of upper-class society in the Regency) rather than historical crises (such as the Napoleonic Wars) provide a context for the situations. The rules of society, which can be interpreted as extreme forms of those which, in less overt ways, were still constraining women's roles during the period in which these books were written, allow the norms of male – female relationships to be explored, challenged and yet ultimately reinforced.

The changed nature of the typical romantic hero is symptomatic of this shift of emphasis. The 'manly' hero of the adventure stories of the 1890s – a young and ingenuous boy or a man of action with few social graces – gave place, after 1926 (the date of Heyer's *These Old Shades*),[4] in the work of Heyer and her followers, to the man of the world who hides his sensitivity under a cynical, even brutal, exterior. Heroines changed less in character, but their function – of challenging the rules of society, in particular the gender roles allotted to men and women – became more important. Cunning and love of power, at first the property of the villain, became associated with the heroes of later romances. These changes were associated with a change of perspective in which the hero moved from object of identification to desirable other. The winning and taming of such a figure were the heroine's triumph, even though his behaviour represented a display of patriarchal power at its most extreme.

The heroine's own pattern of behaviour – to overthrow masculine power in one way, while succumbing to it in another – can be read as a traditionally romantic one, at first denying and then being overcome by the power of Love, personified and seen as godlike. In comparison with medieval and Renaissance romances, however, relatively little attention is paid to the actual falling in love in contemporary romances, much as it may seem a central concern. The behaviour of hero and heroine is used as a signifier for those values of 'private' activity already mentioned: the importance of a particular kind of family life, self-fulfilment and the distribution of power and wealth in society.

Historical romance may be seen as responding to changes in public attitudes in its shift of focus from the public sphere to the private and domestic one. Many of the concerns, however, remain the same. The genre has been able to accommodate some changing attitudes, but ultimately the messages of the texts are backward-looking. They suggest the unchanging nature of values which are essentially those of the period in which the book was written. The means by which such messages operate is through the detailed sets of associations built up by the text.

*

These sets of associations form part of the means by which the romance, with all its extraordinary situations, is made to seem "realistic". The effect does not arise because the text actually mimics actuality, since, as Barthes has pointed out,[5] the carefully placed concrete detail in a novel does not refer to anything which actually exists or has existed; the wine barrel which bursts open on the streets of the Faubourg St Antoine in *A Tale of Two Cities*,[6] for example, is an imaginary one. The reader responds from his or her experience to the connotations of the detail, which thus gains an effect of reality. The effect of verisimilitude is an illusion, created by structural features of the text. The effect is, however, a potent one: the reader is drawn in to accept the imagined world, at least for the moment, as real.

In the case of historical romance, perhaps the most obvious source of verisimilitude is the use of history itself which, as discussed in Chapter 1 (see p.2), is used to validate the story. If the narrative incorporates a good deal of historical details, the impression is given that this is the result of indefatigable scholarly research, and so – of course – true. Some of Janice Radway's respondents (in *Reading the Romance*) clearly believed this: one remarked: 'You don't feel you've got a history lesson, but somewhere in there you have.'[7] This use of imaginary detail to produce an effect of 'fact', however, considerably antedates Radway's 1970s 'bodice-rippers'; it may almost be considered an essential part of the historical novel, since it is found in the work of Scott, and is very noticeable in later nineteenth-century writers such as Ainsworth and Reade, and in novels by more respected writers such as George Eliot's *Middlemarch* (1871), which has references to Wordsworth, Humphry Davy and the Catholic Emancipation Bill. In Scott's *Rob Roy* (1817) the story is dated 'early in the eighteenth century', but the date is soon confirmed by a detailed description of the appropriate period costume of Mr Osbaldistone's clerk (with 'pearl-grey silk stockings' and 'plaited ruffles').[8]

In the typical romance, the romantic situations of the plot comprise narrative motifs which move the story forward, and, in addition, a number of tiny incidents and details which make the reader continually conscious of the historical context in which the story is taking place. Any one of the plots could be broken down into what Umberto Eco, writing of the film *Casablanca* in *The Role of the Reader*[9] has called 'common' and 'intertextual' frames – though in the case of a book, Boris Tomashevski's word 'motif', meaning the smallest unit of plot, might be a better term.[10] 'Common' frames appeal to our normal experience – eating a meal, for example. 'Intertextual' frames (as when 'the hero fights the villain and wins')[11] are stereotyped situations from textual tradition. Clearly, historical romance contains notable examples of the latter.

'Common' motifs are used in the romances in a way peculiar to historical fiction. Though the reference is to situations within the reader's experience, it is often the difference from normality which is stressed. When the servants strew fresh rushes on the floor of a chamber in Dinah Dean's *The Briar Rose* (1986),[12] we know we are not in a modern household. The most trivial events of everyday life are narrated in a detail one would not expect to find in other genres: characters are described dressing, cooking, eating, doing their hair and even having a bath – an enterprise fraught with danger in Frances Lang's *The Filigree Bird* (1981).

The expansiveness arises because such motifs carry the period detail. At the same time, many writers try to assist reader identification by using the consciousness of hero or heroine to make the detail *seem* normal, a technique which Janice Radway has noted and compared to what 'Umberto Eco has aptly called "the technique of the aimless glance"'.[13] Eco believes that the minute descriptions of inessential detail in Fleming's James Bond thrillers function as a trigger to our 'capacity for identification' and necessary suspension of disbelief. It is a technique noted by Janice Radway in her American 'historicals'; 'the narrator's eye lingers lovingly over the objects and accoutrements of pre-electrical living'.

Such descriptions need not be experienced by readers as delaying the action; the detail is presented as part of the character's sub-conscious awareness, taking a natural place in the sequence of his or her thoughts and actions. The beginning of Dinah Dean's *The Briar Rose* illustrates this:

> Kate slipped through the crowd unnoticed, and entered her uncle's house, which was of no great size, but gave an impression of comfortable living, with fine oak panelling and furniture, gleaming from frequent applications of beeswax, which mingled its sweet scent with that of the rushes and a few autumn roses in a bowl on one broad window-sill.

(p.8)

The 'applications of beeswax' suggest the housewife's craft, and there are familiar domestic details – furniture to be proud of, and flowers on the window-sill. At the same time, the rushes (which, as we have been previously informed, are for strewing on the floor), the panelling, and the broadness of the window-sill are more exotic cues, invoking the reader's knowledge of the past to help her recreate the scene and blend the strangeness of the past with the familiarity of her own life. In this way, the reader is invited to experience a period in the past in a way which is easily meaningful to her, but, at the same time, has its own precise individuality; a device to aid identification with the scene.

The importance of 'period' detail is often emphasized by linking it to significant themes and events in the text. Thus, when in Weyman's *Under the Red Robe* (1894) the hero, de Berault, places on Mme de Cochefôret's table 'a white glazed cup, an old-fashioned piece of the second Henry's time' (p.170), it is a reminder of his Breton childhood and an important factor in his return to respectability; when the 'few herrings' of a Parisian supper during the French Revolution, as described by Orczy, are contrasted with 'a cut of your cheese and home-baked bread' as served at the Fisherman's Rest at Dover,[14] the comparison is intended to show the wretched privations which are the direct consequence of revolt. But this detail is authentically 'period' as well.

In such cases the authenticating detail is so interwoven with the action that it is accepted without the reader's noticing what has happened. The detail is presented as though it were what the hero or heroine was half-consciously noticing, occurring naturally in the sequence of thoughts and actions. This functions as an aid to identification since it mimics what we do naturally in picking up information about our current background, even when our thoughts are preoccupied with other matters.

In helping to give the impression that the reader is actually experiencing what the main character is said to be feeling, the device helps to reduce the distance between the reader and the imagined world. It is one of the devices of 'formal realism' characteristic of the novel form; in popular romances of the twentieth century, the devices used are ones which give an impression of reality with the least disruption of the illusion. The reader is given only the information which is available to the character whose viewpoint she shares, the characters are allowed to speak for themselves with the minimum of authorial intrusion, and the narrative time is more or less the same as that of the imagined world. In the romances written after the Second World War the language, too, is relatively modern, not aiming for a particularly archaic effect as, for instance, Sabatini's or Orczy's language does. Rosalind Brunt, for example, has mentioned the 'oral' quality of Barbara Cartland's language, and the success with which she manages to incorporate sufficient information for the reader to construct a mental image while getting on with the story.[15] The style of a lesser-known writer, Dinah Dean, whose *The Briar Rose* is quoted above (see p.20), has something of this quality too, with a scattering of archaisms to invoke the period: "'Mistress Cecy is still above stairs'" is followed by Cecy's "'Oh, there you are, Kate!'"[16]

The total effect is one of authenticity produced by the few archaisms, blended with a style which is familiar enough to be unnoticeable. It is a combination which makes the contemporary historical romance easy to read and aids identification: Pierre Bourdieu has suggested that such identification is only possible when 'specifically artistic effects . . . can be forgotten'.[17] Such an unnoticeable style can carry a potent ideological charge: a point which may be exemplified through a brief analysis of the opening of one of Barbara Cartland's novels, *The Proud Princess* (1976). The plot is set in motion by an episode in which the heroine, Ilona, out riding, comes upon a mysterious group of men conferring together in a clearing of the forest. The leader tells her to go, and leads her horse out of the clearing. As he does so, he kisses her. It is a favourite stock episode in historical romance, given individuality by the specific detail of time, place and situation.

It is such specific details which provide the 'historical' element. An impression of historical authenticity is given by the chapter heading: the date 1872. There are references in the first page to the heroine's Hungarian blood, though the setting is an imaginary country called Dabrozka, evidently a Balkan country between Hungary and Greece. Later in the chapter we learn that Ilona has lived in Paris during the days of the Commune. Thus the imaginary princess and her country are securely placed in a context of real places and historical events.

This information is stated, however, very much *en passant*. The opening describes the heroine 'glancing back', and the object of her glance, 'the broad open steppe with its brilliant green grass richly interspersed with flowers', is immediately given so that the reader can share it. From that point on, the reader is told what the heroine sees, and what her thoughts and feelings are; it is through this reverie that the circumstances of her situation are conveyed. Thus she asks herself, as she is 'galloping wildly' over the steppe, '"Could anything . . . be more frustrating than to go riding accompanied by two elderly army officers and two grooms?"'; and the reader learns through a rare authorial aside that 'It was the Hungarian in her now that made her determined to escape and enjoy the freedom of the wind on her cheeks.' She reflects upon how much she has been looking forward to riding the horses of Dabrozka, brought up in wildness like those of the neighbouring Hungarian plain: a link with the princess, since, like the Dabrozkans, the horses are described as having some Hungarian blood.

In about ten sentences much information has been conveyed: about the identity of the heroine, the country she lives in, the fact that she has lived as an exile and has only recently returned; and, in addition, the country of Dabrozka has been characterized as having strong links with Hungary (so that any associations with which the reader has mentally invested that country can safely be used to build up a picture of Dabrozka), yet with an 'age-old' history of its own going back at least to the Romans.

But more has been conveyed than factual information. Much of the circumstantial detail belongs to what Roland Barthes has called the semic code:[18] a gradual accretion of specific detail which helps to place setting and characters in a network of associations drawn from the reader's experience. Ilona's attitude to her retinue suggests her lack of pomposity, while the description of the horses both emphasizes their untamed freedom and links them to the human inhabitants of Dabrozka by saying that 'like the people' they were more than half-Hungarian. When, a few lines further on, it is remarked that it is Ilona's Hungarian blood which makes her want to enjoy 'the freedom of the wind on her cheeks', a link is established between the heroine and Dabrozka, with both associated with a love of freedom. This triangular set of associations is gradually built up, and is reinforced later in the text: it is an important part of the narrative.

Aladar, the man who kisses Ilona in the forest, identifies himself as the hero by that act to any reader familiar with the conventions of romance. He, too, is drawn into the network of 'freedom/Dabrozka' associations, both by his evident attraction to Ilona and by the first words which Ilona hears from his group, which are 'fight' and 'injustice'. They suggest, more specifically, a political dimension to his association with freedom; and Ilona is in turn drawn into this by the fact that as she rides back, having rejoined her retinue, she reflects with concern that the peasants no longer sing. This mystery is resolved by the revelation of the harsh attitude of her father, the King of Dabrozka, to his people. The stage is set for Ilona and Aladar to combine in leading an insurrection against her father's tyranny.

Such a rebellion, with its associations of freedom, a renewal of justice, and a care for the people on the lowest rung of the social ladder, is clearly presented as a good thing. What the reader of the story may take to be natural because they can agree with it happily, since the aristocratic status of hero and heroine is to be expected in a romance, is the limitation of revolutionary activism to the country's 'natural' leaders, the nobility. The horror of what happens when the people take up their own cause is suggested by the description of Ilona's sufferings in the Paris Commune, part of her reverie as she is at the same time noticing the silence of the peasants.

In *The Proud Princess* real and invented history and a romantic story blend together to suggest a utopian solution to the social problems of an imaginary country. It seems radical in concerning itself with the needs of the lowest social group in the country, but it is based on an acceptance of the status quo. At the end of the book the peasants, still peasants, have become 'free' again and doubtless will soon begin to sing while they work.

Freedom – presented as having something to do with riding over endless plains with the wind in one's hair, dancing the tarantella in gypsy encampments, and in general doing what one wants, within limits, without a cross father figure to tell one not to – is an important concept in the novel. It is embodied in Ilona's impatience of stuffy protocol, in Aladar's aspirations for his people, and in the gypsies who aid the revolutionaries and who desire only to come and go as they please.

Such aspirations are limited by a consciousness of responsibility on the part of Ilona and Aladar, or a withdrawal from power on the part of the gypsies, who are pleased to acknowledge Ilona's authority. If they are not so limited it can become the vicious individualism represented by the tyrant king or the brigands who, as his tools, kidnap Ilona later in the story. Freedom can therefore be seen as a willing submission to a caring and responsible authority. It is this which is seen as the key to a happy and prosperous society.

The concept, never explicitly stated, is expressed through the gradual building up of a network of *semes*, so that the reader's favourable attitude to the main characters, and to such subordinate figures as the gypsies, is based upon their relationship to freedom – a quality which in turn is assumed to be good because it is related to sympathetic characters.

In fact, 'freedom' is the sum total of a number of characteristics of hero, heroine and related characters, and an explicit definition of it would show it to be a very selective interpretation of the general concept with which the reader is familiar. As a basis for political organization it provides a solution which could be seen to be full of contradictions if it were ever exposed by becoming explicit; but since it never is, the reader can accept it as ideal.

'Realism' and 'history' together, then, validate the romantic elements, but in so doing the 'realism' of the texts invites a reading of both romantic and historical situations which involves an identification with specific social and political values; it may be the assent to these, rather than the details of either the romantic story or, in this case, the invented history, which may be remembered as 'true' by the reader. The values seem all the more relevant since they are seen to operate not only in the invented situation but also, through the way in which the invented history is dovetailed into real events (the Paris Commune, in this case), in the 'real' world as well.

*

The role of 'history' (in the form of selected historical facts) in helping to validate attitudes suggested by the text and making them seem applicable to the real world is thus an important one in these books. This is why novels which on the surface seem to be more concerned with the serious construction of a picture of the past can have much the same effect as a romantic invention such as *The*

Proud Princess. The use of detail in Conan Doyle's *The White Company* (1891), for instance, seems at first sight to be operating in a totally different way from the cues in *The Proud Princess*. What has been said above about the way in which Cartland and other contemporary romance writers use the devices of realism seems inoperative in Conan Doyle's novel: the very beginning, which offers not an introduction to a main character but two scale maps of the area in which the action is to take place, suggests a textbook rather than a novel. The maps, however, are not referred to in the text, and their importance is rather that of Barthes' 'concrete detail' which signifies not itself but 'the real'.[19]

The impression of a history textbook is reinforced by the first chapter. There is no immediate sense of identification with any of the characters: the implied reader, in Iser's term,[20] is set at some distance from the imagined world. A bird's-eye view of southern England, from 'Peat-cutters on Blackdown' to 'fishers upon the Exe', is first given, before the focus is narrowed to the district around Beaulieu Abbey and finally to the chamber in which its abbot is awaiting the arrival of the monks. The time-scale, too, presents some problems, fluctuating between a general period in which the Abbey bell was 'a common sound' and a more specific one 'within the memory of old lay-brother Athanasius' which stretches back to 'the year after the battle of Bannockburn' (a historical detail which helps to define the temporal context and relate it to a real event), and finally settling on a particular moment when 'the shadows were neither short nor long', the bell was ringing and the abbot pacing his chamber.

The effect is disorientating, particularly since the author digresses to describe the arrival of the monks to answer the call of the bell, a description which includes a flashback to the previous evening when they were summoned. The only concessions to the reader's expectations of novelistic convention are some phrases which function as part of Barthes' hermeneutic code:[21] 'Why should the great bell of Beaulieu ring?' or 'so urgent a message', which presumably are intended to keep the reader mystified and in suspense.

The greater part of this opening, however, is taken up by a description of the Beaulieu monks, who arrive carrying spades or shearing tools, or 'spotted with grape-juice', as though they had broken off suddenly from what they were doing. The signs of their labour combine to give a picture of the diversity of monkish occupation, and so to suggest the central importance of the monastery in medieval economy. The picture compensates to some extent for what follows, an episode in which a young novice is expelled who has offended against the absurd conventions of the monastic rule – by such 'innocent' and 'natural' behaviour as helping a woman across a stream, for instance – in which the monastery appears in a bad light, with suggestions of creating an over-intellectualized élite separated and protected from the realities of medieval life.

The effect of such a beginning upon the reader is likely to be an impression that, even though the episode is actually invented by the author, its ingredients are factual and the presentation neutral: 'history', rather than 'romance', in fact. Yet, of course, the impression of balance and neutrality is illusory. History retold is an imaginative construct, just as narrative is, and in the case of historical romance, where the plot is made up so largely of traditional situations, the historical element may paradoxically provide the most inventive element. The *impression* is, however, that it is the detailed historical picture which is true; and the effect of placing such a description side by side with an invented episode is to suggest that the author is well aware of the possibility of bias in invented episodes and is providing compensatory evidence which leaves the reader free to make up his or her own mind about what is likely to be the truth.

Once the reader is embarked on the scene of the novice's trial, balance and neutrality can be happily forgotten. The *semes* associated with monks and novice function in much the same way as they do in *The Proud Princess*. Thus, the novice, Hordle John, is presented as almost aggressively 'natural', with his thick muscular arms covered with reddish down (like a fox's hide?) and giving an impression of bursting from his clothes, his cowl thrown back and the gown unfastened, its skirts looped up to allow his legs free play and his arms 'protruded' from the sleeves. He appears to be an attractive character, with independence and good nature suggested by his 'half-humorous, half-defiant' expression.

The abbot, by contrast, is all repression. In 'crushing . . . passions' he had 'crushed himself', wrote Conan Doyle; and the impression is reinforced through the semic code by such details as his 'long white nervous hands' and 'thin thought-worn features' which suggest that this long repression of his natural instincts has wasted him physically.

These semic associations are set to work to build up a picture of Hordle John, with his 'broad West Saxon drawl', as English and manly, as opposed to the monks who, though 'English to a man', accept without question 'the Anglo-French dialect used in religious houses'; the impression is given that they have sold out to an alien system, though the dialect is to be expected as a feature of what was probably a Norman foundation. The detail is needed, however, to throw the Englishness of John into relief: it is the first stage in the construction of an equation of 'England = warfare = natural = good' which is an important strand in the ideology of the novel.

*

Although it is the formal realist conventions which thus carry the ideology of the novels, specifically through the operation of the semic code, the history is an important element in the reader's experience and helps the reader to 'swallow' ideologically charged material unawares.

This is true whether it is the historical element which is fore-grounded, as in *The White Company*, or the romantic element, as in *The Proud Princess*. None the less, it remains true that at the core of all the novels is a collection of romantic situations which themselves can be symbolically interpreted and so carry their own ideological messages. What happens when the symbolic interpretation of situation and character relationship runs counter to that of the historical contextual detail?

This can be seen to happen in *The Proud Princess*, for example, in the symbolic suggestions of female subordination contained in the relationship between the masterful Aladar and Ilona – suggestions first adumbrated in the kiss which Aladar gives to Ilona in the clearing and his reference to her as 'you little fool' (she does not reply with anything comparable – such as 'you big lummock'). These seem to run counter to all the ideas of freedom and their association with Ilona which are so important in the 'historical' dimension of the novel.

In the same way, what happens when the equation 'Hordle John (peasant) = English = natural = good', set up by the first episode of *The White Company*, collides with the romantic need to centre the action in the adventures of a young aristocrat? In both books, the needs of the romance seem to run counter to the messages given by the historical detail of the text.

A historical romance may thus be seen as comprising two systems of signification which to some extent run counter to and undermine each other. It is the effect of this upon the message of the text which will be the focus of attention in the following chapters.

Chapter 3

The readers of historical romance

The operation of the signifying systems described in Chapter 2 depends on the ways in which the reader mobilizes his or her experience, both of texts and of 'real life', to 'concretize' (in Iser's term) and add meaning to the cues provided by the words on the page. The 'message' thus not only contributes to but arises from the way in which the readers construct their world-picture, and this is in turn dependent upon their location within society in terms of class, culture, gender, time and place.

It is therefore pertinent to enquire about the nature of the social group to which historical romances have made and do make their appeal. In the case of the earlier books this enquiry presents difficulties. Claud Cockburn complained in *Bestseller* that for books in this period (the late nineteenth and early twentieth centuries), 'accurate statistics of total *sales* are hard to come by, and of total readership there are no statistics'.[1] He argues for a middle-class readership for his best-sellers through examining the numbers and prices of the various editions and comparing these with what people were likely to pay: a reasonable procedure to some extent, as long as its limitations are recognized, since circumstances can alter the amounts which people are willing to pay for books – a book-buyer might happily pay more for something intended as a present, for example, than for something to while away the time on a railway journey.

When evidence of this kind about the readership of historical romance – much of which reached the best-seller lists at the turn of the century – is compared with information about book-buying and reading habits from other sources, such as that supplied by David Altick in *The English Common Reader* (1957), a reasonably consistent and likely picture of the genre's readership in the early years of this century begins to emerge.

Cockburn assumed that the comparatively vast readership of best-sellers in the Edwardian and late Victorian periods was drawn largely from the 'British Mandarinate', since this formed the 'bulk' of the novel-buying and novel-borrowing public.[2] By this he seems to have had in mind what François Bédarida termed the 'upper crust' of the bourgeoisie, which comprised the wealthiest bankers, merchants and manufacturers, and members of 'gentlemanly' professions such as the Law and the Church – that is, those with incomes ranging from about £800 to £5,000 per year.[3] It is true that Stanley Weyman seemed to have had middle-class readers in mind since, accordingly to Altick, some of the periodicals in which his work was serialized catered particularly for this class during the period. On the other hand, their nature does not necessarily suggest an upper-middle-class readership of the kind Cockburn had in mind: the kind of education demanded by the books and the periodicals in which they appeared, as well as the prices at which they sold, would have been within the command of a wider band of readers, including the 'lower middle class', defined by Bédarida as comprising small shopkeepers, bank clerks, office workers, school-masters, and similar 'white collar' workers such as salesmen and railway workers; to these might be added skilled workers who earned between £80 and £90 a year in the late nineteenth century, and who had had some education.[4]

Some idea of the kind of reader to whom Weyman and Conan Doyle's books made their appeal may be gained from the readership of the periodicals in which they were serialized. *The Cornhill Magazine*, for instance, in which Weyman had work serialized, was, according to David Altick, a new kind of periodical introduced to fill a gap between the high-brow *Athenaeum* – a monthly which retailed at two shillings in the mid-century, rising to two-and-sixpence by its end – and the low-brow weekly *London Journal*, considered by Altick to have made its appeal to the working class. The *Cornhill* retailed at a shilling, which meant that readers who had been unable to afford higher-priced magazines such as *Blackwood's* could buy it.[5] Conan Doyle's *The White Company* was also serialized in the *Cornhill*. Other periodicals in which their work appeared, such as the *Leisure Hour*, were of a similar nature; the *Leisure Hour* was published by a religious publishing house, but Altick points out that its contents differed very little from those of 'secular' periodicals and it probably attracted the same kind of readership.[6] The general picture Altick gives is of a family readership, with fair but not large incomes, who enjoyed fiction of a more serious kind than the melodramas provided by, say, the *London Journal*.

What has been said of Weyman and Conan Doyle is true also of other historical romancers, such as A. E. W. Mason. Some of his work was published by Macmillan in their six-shilling series: these books, cheap editions of popular works, are some evidence both of popularity and of a relatively prosperous readership, since they were not addressed to the poorest readers as the shilling and two-and-sixpenny reprints were.[7]

This, too, confirms the picture of a middle-class, family readership. It may, perhaps, be specified further. Both David Altick[8] and Raymond Williams[9] have written of a new class which was developing, and increasing in literacy and buying power, at the end of the century – the time when Weyman, Conan Doyle and the others were beginning to write. Though some of these owned shops or small businesses,[10] many, like the working class, sold their labour for hire, but their labour was of a skilled kind. So, of course, was that of many manual workers who served apprenticeships, but while these received their training at the workplace the new class received it within the traditional educational system. This was the class of public servants – clerks and teachers, for instance.[11]

David Thomson[12] has argued that it was these readers who provided the taste for exotic adventure which cloak-and-dagger novels, among others, helped to fulfil. The members of the rapidly growing public services – the Civil Service, becoming notably enlarged during the period between 1890 and the outbreak of the Second World War, and the bureaucracy of an expanding Local Government – together with the clerks and the shop assistants whose numbers had been growing thoughout the century, and who were also frequently drawn from the ranks of the lower-middle class, were newly influential through the sheer size of their social group.

Thomson describes their lives as all 'semi-gentility and conventional monotony; bank clerks and shop assistants, factory managers and lesser civil servants, armies of them just adjusting themselves to a pinched and colourless existence'.[13] He notes their taste for adventure stories such as those by Kipling; historical adventure stories, so like these in spirit, can be seen as equally providing this class with glamour and excitement. They continued to appear on the best-seller lists during the early decades of the twentieth century.

The prices for best-sellers of the 1930s, appended by Q. D. Leavis to *Fiction and the Reading Public* (1932), suggest a very similar readership to that of the 1890s romances, even though the prices had, of course, risen considerably; and, in addition, the fact that books by Orczy and Sabatini eventually appeared in paperback to be carried home with the shopping, as Leavis suggests, widened the scope of the readership. None the less such books needed to develop the popularity which made it worthwhile to bring out paperback versions, and this popularity was presumably created by those of a slightly higher spending power.[14]

To suggest that the lower middle class and, in particular, the public servants and representatives of minor professions, composed the readership for historical romance in this period is thus to oversimplify the picture. It would be wrong, too, to suggest that any such group holds an easily identifiable set of attitudes and beliefs. None the less, evidence suggests that such readers did form a core of a public which enjoyed such stories and presumably found their concerns addressed to some extent within them.

Also, the texts themselves are written from different individual standpoints: Conan Doyle, for example, a campaigner against instances of social injustice, shows much more interest in the welfare of the 'commons' than a romancer such as A. E. W. Mason.

Despite these provisos, historical romances written between the 1890s and the Second World War do draw upon a network of associations which suggest an identifiable system of values and attitudes. Indeed, an overview of the texts suggests a more coherent value system than is likely to have existed in fact. As Roger Bromley has written of texts dealing with the more recent past in this period, they 'make unitary and coherent a fragmentary and contradictory collection of ideas and opinions'.[15] Such articulation is likely to have the effect of confirming as 'common sense' a number of vaguely formulated attitudes.

The narratives speak to attitudes which in many cases are recognizably middle-class: the grounding of the narrative in the middle and upper classes while showing the actions of the commons as peripheral, even aberrant, as Conan Doyle or Mason do, is an instance. This is not a case of simple reflection: the function of the narrative motifs is often compensatory, but it is compensating for concerns, anxieties and frustrations which recognizably arise from the British experience at this period, and, in particular, from the experience of that segment of society from which, it has been argued, the historical-romance-reading public has been drawn.

*

One or two general points can be made first about attitudes throughout the century between 1890 and 1990, and about the experiences from which these attitudes arose.

The most general point is that the kind of social change which was part of the process of industrialization in the early part of the nineteenth century – for instance the growth of towns, technological developments which began to affect every area of life, and associated changes in social relationships – did not come to a halt but continued and, if anything, accelerated during this period. The effect upon everyday life was to give a sense of sharp division between the 'modernity' of the contemporary world and the traditional society of the past.

The effect of such a sense can be to lead people towards an overvaluation of a particular vision of the past. Patrick Wright, drawing upon Agnes Heller's concept of 'everyday life', has noted this disruptive effect of modernity, characterized by a sense of disjunction with a stable past and of belonging to a society which 'looks forward along the perspectives of a dream of progress which itself seems progressively deranged'.[16] In a present which seems to be in a constant process of transformation, the '"sense of historical existence" becomes progressively anxious, searching more intently for answers which – in the dislocated experience of modernity – seem to be less and less readily forthcoming'.[17]

Secondly, although in general during the past century life for most people was becoming more prosperous and comfortable, despite social inequality, the century has been one of relative economic decline for Britain. David Thomson has characterized the 1890s as a period of prosperity sandwiched between two periods of depression,[18] but it was a qualified prosperity: the newly federalized states of Germany and America were beginning to threaten Britain's steel industry, for example.[19] On the other hand, Arthur Marwick has pointed out that, even with her 'economic primacy' challenged by Germany and America, Britain in 1900 still 'had the world's trade at her feet',[20] and new colonies were producing new sources of raw materials. In 1900, Britain's share of world trade was 35 per cent;[21] by 1913 it was 25 per cent; and by 1938 19 percent,[22] since when it has come down to single figures.

Pride in economic leadership therefore necessarily gave place to an uncomfortable sense of dwindling national power over the century as a whole. It has been suggested that compensating attitudes have developed – indeed, Martin Weiner[23] has suggested that one reason for the decline was an undervaluing of manufacturing and money-making, seen in the 'gentrification' of the manufacturers and financiers, and an over-valuing of leisure which affected all classes in society. If this is a controversial view,[24] some historians have seen the British accommodation to new circumstances as being relatively calm: François Bédarida believed that in the 1970s the English valued an 'English brand of happiness – leisurely, relaxed, sheltered, not over-strenuous', which would have been anathema to the 'tough conquering race of earlier days'.[25] If there were indeed such changes in attitude, they have been challenged since the 1970s; and they are not, in any case, incompatible with a sense of loss.

There were other sources for this as well as economic decline and changes in 'everyday life'. In the 1890s, for instance, Britain was still taking part in a race for new colonies,[26] and in 1900 'bold red patches' were 'spread over the globe'[27] to be a source of pride. After 1918 the Empire covered 'an area hitherto unsurpassed' after Britain secured mandates over former German and Turkish colonies,[28] but transformations in the nature of the Empire, with countries like Canada and Australia gaining Dominion status, meant that Britain was no longer all-powerful within it. After the Second World War came a much more complete process of decolonization, and though, as Bédarida pointed out, this process proceeded fairly quietly, 'it was hard to get used to being confined within 90,000 square miles'.[29]

*

Such were the continuities which provided a framework for the attitudes of historical romance readers between 1890 and 1990. Attitudes were also affected by circumstances more specific to particular periods within the century: the two world wars are obvious examples. Moreover, attitudes and beliefs often have a residual life after the circumstances which gave birth to them have begun to pass away. Thus in the 1890s, when any precariousness in Britain's economic prestige was in any case masked to some extent by the importance of the British Empire, the existence of which could be seen as a source of national pride as well as an opportunity for the individual Briton to find economic and social advancement,

Britain could be seen as bringing to less favoured nations the advantages of democratic government, greater industrial prosperity and more individual freedom for the masses who came under the beneficent rule of British law – what Hall *et al.* refer to as a 'civilizing burden' which gave a 'quiet, unspoken' assumption of English superiority.[30]

François Bédarida, analysing this assumption, ascribed it in part to 'Industrialism, Protestantism, liberalism, the three great forces of the age'.[31] These three strands were tightly interwoven, and their moral aspects had a profound effect on the British view of their national character, even though by the 1890s all three were to some extent under threat. For many people they must still have combined to form a set of unexamined assumptions. It is worthwhile, therefore, to give a brief explanation of each strand, each of which has its roots in the Victorian period.

William Ashworth saw the last quarter of the nineteenth century as a time when 'the most onerous stage of investment in industrialization was over',[32] and the country was enjoying the fruits of this in the form of greater prosperity. The British had good reason to suppose, therefore, that they were natural leaders in manufacturing as well as in trade, though as Arthur Marwick has pointed out, industry 'continued to thrive on old products and old methods', and supremacy in some of the new industries such as chemicals was taken from the start by Germans and Americans.[33] In Victorian England it was the middle classes who had been 'the standard bearers of industrialism'.[34] This rather vague class description is glossed by Bédarida according to 'three relatively precise criteria . . . the consciousness of a common identity . . . a certain type of occupation . . . a comfortable standard of living',[35] to which he adds 'a degree of education'. Although he pointed out that the middle classes comprised 'a jigsaw puzzle' of varied groups, he distinguished three broad divisions, the 'upper crust' and 'lower middle class' described above (see p.30) and the 'true bourgeoisie', the 'middle middle class',[36] composed of industrialists, professionals, managers and senior clerks in government service.

All these subdivisions, including that from which, it has been argued, many of the readers of historical romance were drawn (see p.30), were imbued with some common attitudes. 'Protestantism' gave rise to some of the most characteristic – especially since, despite a fair number of Anglicans amongst their ranks, the majority were Nonconformist. Temperance, chastity, the home and the family were all highly valued.[37] Hard work and bold entrepreneur-ship were virtues: 'success in business was a sign of divine favour'.[38] Hence, it could be argued that the inequalities of society were divinely sanctioned, or at least the work of nature, and impossible to change.

It was 'natural', too, that women should be subordinate to men in the family, but in recompense they were considered in many ways superior to men – Coventry Patmore's 'angel in the house':[39] man's inspiration, a civilizing influence, and the fount of the family virtues. At the same time, they were considered deficient in such 'masculine' qualities as creative ingenuity, endurance and adven-turousness, all of which were highly valued qualities during the period, so that women were 'exalted and put down at the same time'.[40]

Even though the main foundation of such attitudes, middle-class Protestantism, was itself coming under threat in the late Victorian period from such influences as rationalism, science, and a growing apathy towards religion,[41] the attitudes themselves were strongly held throughout the Victorian period. In the 1890s they were beginning to be challenged: by workers' unrest, leading to a series of strikes,[42] which George Dangerfield explained with reference to 'a certain conscious security . . . the workers did not want to be safe any more . . . they had been repressed too long';[43] and by the beginnings of the women's suffrage movement, which was to gain strength and become of primary significance in the following de-cade.[44] But such challenges were not likely to change general attitudes; rather, it was more likely that their effect was to cause them to be more articulated and held more strongly and defensively.

The third strand of 'English superiority', liberalism, refers not so much to a political party as to an attitude of mind; one which placed a high value upon liberty, interpreted as the right to personal freedoms such as freedom of speech, freedom from imprisonment without trial, and freedom to enjoy one's own property.[45] Other ingredients were individualism and *laissez-faire*. Like the other strands, liberalism was challenged in the 1890s. During this decade the wide divisions between rich and poor became the focus of attention, with the publication of surveys such as that by Charles Booth of pauperism in the 1890s; and these years also saw the beginnings of that programme of welfare reform which was to culminate in the building of the welfare state. A liberal historian such as David Thomson, writing in the still-expansive years of the 1950s, could show this as undoubted progress.[46]

'New' liberals such as L. T. Hobhouse and J. A. Hobson reinterpreted some of the old arguments for individualism and *laissez-faire*, such as Herbert Spencer's analogy between society and a living organism,[47] as support for a 'balanced, regulated society' with the state as arbiter.[48] Such an interventionalist view of the state was far from palatable to many liberals: A. V. Dicey, for example, was to look back with nostalgia to the individualism of the mid-nineteenth century when individual energy could flourish untrammelled by any consideration apart from respect for the liberties of others,[49] and Spencer himself warned of the dangers of too strong a state.[50]

The 1890s was a time, therefore, when traditional attitudes of mind were beginning to come under threat, and voices were being raised in their defence. The ordinary member of the bourgeoisie, however, was likely to be still 'saturated' by them.[51] Though many doubtless saw that changes brought about by the new liberalism, such as the new welfare services, were useful and necessary, ingrained habits of thought were likely to make them aware at the same time of the dangers of being over-regulated.

Against such a background, the historical romances of the period, which exalted individual prowess, the greatness of England, and English liberal virtues, made an obvious appeal. Historical adventure stories of this time, too, such as those written by Stanley Weyman, provided images of 'just' states which yet protected individual freedoms. In this way the books could offer a resolution for the contradictions in such opposed attitudes.

*

This might explain the dominance of the genre of historical romance at the turn of the century, when Stanley Weyman was the leading author.[52] The danger was that the genre, too suited to its time, might not have survived the changes which were to follow in the new century. In fact there is considerable continuity between the work of Weyman – who, indeed, went on writing until 1927 – and that of younger writers such as Rafael Sabatini and Baroness Orczy. At the same time there are changes: heroes are less involved in 'history' than Weyman and Conan Doyle made theirs, and a new kind of idyllic romance began to be produced by writers such as Maurice Hewlett, Jeffrey Farnol and, later, Warwick Deeping.[53]

These developments are understandable if seen against a back-ground of changing circumstances. In the Edwardian period this meant chiefly the presages of a coming war. Arthur Marwick has commented upon the 'extreme jingoism' which accompanied the Boer War, adding that for realists at this time war – 'in a world in which Germany was challenging Britain's commercial and naval supremacy', and France, too, had been regarded as a potential enemy until the Entente of 1904 – was 'practically an inevitability'.[54]

There was unrest, too, in society: the activities of the Women's Social and Political Union, founded to promote the interests of the 'suffragettes' by deeds as well as words, brought into the women's suffrage debate an element of violence which intensified after 1910; and between 1910 and 1912 there was a wave of strikes on the railways, in the docks, and amongst miners and cotton operatives amongst others, some of which were also attended by violence.[55] There was certainly enough unrest to provide the anxieties which, Claud Cockburn believed,[56] sent readers to the idyllic romances of writers such as Jeffrey Farnol, to live in imagination in a world without public conflict.

*

Despite the fact that adventurous romance of this kind continued to be published after the First World War – Sabatini, for instance, found his greatest success in the 'twenties and was still publishing work in 1949[57] – its great vogue had past. Books by established authors continued to find readers, but as they retired there were no others to take their place. And though best-selling authors con-tinued to produce the kind of book which had given them their reputation, what was lacking was the second rank of historical fiction writers like Claud Cockburn's uncle, who, in the 1890s, had been able to make a steady living from historical fiction without ever achieving best-seller status.[58]

It was during this period that the shift in audience already mentioned began to take place. Georgette Heyer, who did so much to establish historical romance as a women's genre, has left evidence in the form of letters about sales and fan mail from her readers, of whose nature and numbers she was very well aware. It is evident from her increased sales that she, having begun her career as a moderately successful writer of 'swashbucklers' in 1921, had begun to tap a new market in 1925 with the publication of *These Old Shades*. *The Black Moth* of 1921 had been written in the first place for a sick brother,[59] and it centres around a hero who, in true boy's story tradition, has been blackballed from good society because he has taken the blame for an episode of card-cheating involving his brother. The story is full of adventures, with a good deal of fighting. Although *These Old Shades* contains some adventure, it deals chiefly with the relationship between the Duke of Avon and his ward, with whom he has fallen in love. Its focus on personal relationships makes it more suited to a female readership than the mixed one of earlier books, and this, it seemed, was the audience it in fact tapped. It was a readership which stayed with her for the rest of her career as long as she kept to the precise formula of which *These Old Shades* was a prototype

Heyer's was a market which contained some men – her biographer, Jane Aiken Hodge, refers to dons and journalists, many of whom were male – but which was predominantly female. Hodge divides Heyer's readers into two groups, a smaller one which included the dons and journalists as well as 'intelligent women everywhere', and the 'great fan public', which was predominantly female and middle-class.[60]

The market which had developed for Heyer was not satisfied with one woman's *oeuvre*. Other writers of women's romance were beginning to realize the potential of historical fiction for women. What seems to have happened is that historical fiction of the Heyer type was gradually subsumed into the general field of women's romance. Indeed, there is some evidence to suggest that Heyer became influential in creating a definitive formula for women's romance in general as it was produced from the 1920s onwards. The character of the hero, saturnine and abrasive, and his position of wealth and authority, for instance, are typical of the genre, as Ann Rosalind Jones points out.[61] Though similar heroes had of course been found in romance since the heyday of the Gothic novel in the eighteenth century, Heyer may indeed have been instrumental in providing the definitive ingredients for the formula. In this connection, it is interesting to note that Heyer's first publishers were not Heinemann, with whom her name is more usually associated, but those quintessential publishers of women's romantic fiction, Mills & Boon. To them, Heyer is not so much a historical novelist as a 'romantic fiction author'.[62] It seems, therefore, as though the market for Heyer-type romance was in many respects that for women's romantic fiction in general – that is, for romance with a contemporary setting as well as historical fiction.

At least some of Heyer's readers - those characterized by Hodge as enjoying the 'hard core of realism' under the 'syllabub'[63] – may well have been uninterested in the work of plagiarists and successors whose work was geared specifically to the romantic market. They liked the detail of the historical setting, the comedy of manners and the often quite allusive wit of the style, as much as they enjoyed the love story.

Those readers who moved from the books of Heyer to those of her imitators must have been primarily loyal to the love-element, since that is the one thing all the books have in common besides their historical setting. This suggests that the audience for the imitators is very close to that for women's romance in general; and it is evident from surveys of women's romance readers that the readership for this genre, including modern historical romance, is drawn predominantly from the working class. Peter Mann's analysis of the Euromonitor survey for 1983,[64] for example, shows the readership for romantic fiction in general (which, presumably, he thinks includes historical romance, since it is not given a separate category) 'to be strongly skewed towards the working class, with over two-thirds of the readership being in the C(2)DE group' of the Registrar General's classification: that is, roughly, groups which contained skilled, semi-skilled and unskilled workers, though Mann remarks that his analysis shows there to be an appreciable lower-middle-class element of office workers, shop workers and teachers.

This 'skew' towards the working class may well account for some elements of the contemporary historical romances. Heyer's romances are intertextual in the sense that they draw upon a reader's familiarity with older novels of the mainstream, in particular those of Jane Austen. In *Regency Buck*, for example, the heroine's comments on *Pride and Prejudice* (by 'a lady') show her to have an intelligent taste, while allowing the reader the pleasure of imagining how a well-known text was first received. This awareness of Regency writing has affected the style of the books, which draws attention to itself in a way that the style of the later romantic texts does not. The beginning of *The Quiet Gentleman* (1951) is typical:

> In the guide-books it figured as Stanyon Castle; on the tongues of the villagers it was the Castle; the Polite World spoke of it as Stanyon, as it spoke of Woburn, and of Chevely. It was situated in Lincolnshire, not very many miles from Grantham, rather nearer to Stamford: a locality considered by those who were more

interested in the chase than in any particular grandeur or scenery to be admirable.[65]

The parallel main clauses of the first sentence are matched by parallel phrases in the second, to give an effect of formality which is rather like the style of the Regency guidebook it seems at times to be imitating ('Later generations had enlarged and beautified the structure' or 'A medieval fortress . . . had previously stood on the site').[66] It gives the impression of something to be savoured to some extent as parody, and so implies practice in reading older 'classic' texts; contemporary romances in general are more 'readerly', as Janice Radway and Rosalind Brunt have both remarked,[67] and their area of intertextual reference is within the genre of contemporary romance itself – that is, when the heroine sometimes reflects that her adventures are like those in a romance.

Whether the *social* messages of the text are so very different is a different matter. Clearly, the experience of women from different classes varied very considerably during the period between the 1920s and the present, but there were areas of experience which affected them similarly, and these are the areas which are foregrounded as primary concerns in the novels – both those of Heyer and those of later writers.

In many ways women seemed to be offered wider opportunities during this period. Their political aspirations were already becoming a focus of concern during the 1890s and this concern developed during the early years of the twentieth century, alongside a sense that such aspirations were associated with an 'unfeminine' violence. Though both world wars saw an increase in jobs for women, with women entering areas of work previously closed to them, even during the war they did so with a sense in many cases that they were sacrificing their 'natural' aspirations towards domesticity and, as Denise Riley has shown,[68] there was pressure after each war on them to return to the home to safeguard the jobs of returning soldiers.

In the 1920s the 'flapper' might have seemed more independent than girls of her mother's generation had been, but David Thomson has remarked that such changes were superficial and, in any case, only affected a small proportion of women.[69] Though the pattern of women's lives has changed during the century, with work coming to be seen as a natural stage before marriage, or, later, in the period between marriage and starting a family, and with increasing numbers of older married women returning to the workforce, for the majority of women career aspirations have remained subordinate to domestic responsibilities, which are still seen as their concern.

The images of women presented by the early adventure stories suggest the possibility that male readers and authors may have felt indications of widening horizons (even if to some extent illusory) to be a threat. Women may occasionally be allowed a brave action, as when Bonne de Villeneuve cuts the bonds of her lover, tied to a galloping horse, in *The Abbess of Vlaye* (1904) by Stanley Weyman. She faints, however, immediately afterwards, and the action is consequently easy to reconcile with her femininity, which has already been established by the way in which she keeps the peace in her home and makes sure the household is properly maintained. The romances of women writers from the 1920s onwards foreground the roles of women in society, seeing this as a problematic area, but offering resolutions which suggest inconsistent apprehensions of female needs: the heroine is allowed to question the conventions of society, but only within limits, and in the end is forced to conform – and to enjoy conforming.

In all its aspects, the representation of society in the novels is congruent with the use of cultural forms as an instrument of bourgeois hegemony described by Alan Swingewood, by which 'the bourgeoisie seeks to dominate society through its own institutions built upon parliamentary democracy and a free market economy and thus achieves legitimation not through force but through consent'.[70] Historical romances in the century between 1890 and 1990 may have occasionally questioned the values of their society, but in general they constructed a picture of past society which showed it as evolving the institutions which would keep the dangers and unfairnesses of a market economy in check. In this construction such concepts as freedom, self-development and the natural, as opposed to the socially constructed, are of crucial importance.

This image of the past was created to support a view of society which could be confused and self-contradictory. It is scarcely surprising, therefore, that the image itself was full of contradictions, which analysis shows clearly. How that image was created, and the kind of cue which was offered for interpretation by the kind of reader described above, will be the subject of the following chapters.

Chapter 4

Evolution versus revolution
The inevitability of the bourgeois state

The image of the state and its institutions has been reflected in historical romances since the time of Scott, though more recent female-centred romance makes little more than passing reference to the political settings. Although the historical romances from the 1890s and the earlier half of the twentieth century are concerned with exciting adventures, however, these are always set within a political context. *The Scarlet Pimpernel* (1905) revolves around the French Revolution, and so does Rafael Sabatini's *Scaramouche* (1921), while A. E. W. Mason's heroes in *Lawrence Clavering* (1897) and *Clementina* (1901) are Jacobites working on behalf of the Old Pretender against the Hanoverian state. This means that even though the books are not *about* politics, they nevertheless give a picture of a political situation in what purports to be a specific historical moment.

Inevitably, questions such as the nature of government, the role of the state and the distribution of power in society are fore-grounded, even if no explicit statement is made about them. The image of government presented is pre-eminently progressive: in-stitutions are shown in the course of development towards a fair, tolerant and representative system of government. Though this course may have an occasional hiatus, active intervention is shown to be counter-productive because it cuts across the delicate web of factors which will in the end produce a 'modern' government. But although such government is supposed to be based on 'freedom', power is inevitably shown to be the prerogative of a ruling class: the course of development is in reality towards the 'bourgeois hegemony' as formulated by Swingewood, quoted in the previous chapter (see p.42). The texts therefore imply approval of tendencies favouring such a state. One of these could be revolution – but only if it could be shown to be necessary, and safely in the past. This is the attitude attributed to Burke in Robert Coll's account of the development of a liberal concept of the state.[1] Colls argues that the attitude was common at the end of the nineteenth century, and influenced liberal interpretation of political history.

Those who took this attitude might believe that revolution was sometimes necessary to preserve traditional freedoms, but that in itself it was a terrible thing, leading to the rule of the mob – Matthew Arnold's dangerous 'populace'.[2] In the romances written in the 1890s and 1900s, such as those by Weyman, Conan Doyle, Orczy and Sabatini, sympathetic attitudes towards revolution are tempered by images of its horror which recall Carlyle and Dickens. The populace, once it begins to reach out for power, is portrayed as a mob, its members less than fully human and needing the firm control of the traditional ruling class.

Revolution is shown as necessary in these texts when the ruling class abrogates its responsibilities. 'Good' members of the ruling class are aware of the needs of the people they govern – which include being ruled with a necessary firmness. Their qualities, though displaced into the past, are essentially those of a Victorian gentleman as described by Marc Girouard in *The Return to Camelot*.[3]

All these attitudes can be exemplified in three novels from the period between 1890 and 1910: Sir Arthur Conan Doyle's *The White Company*, Stanley Weyman's *The Abbess of Vlaye* (1904), and Rafael Sabatini's *The Trampling of the Lilies*. In these novels, it is possible to detect individual differences of attitude, but there is a general similarity which suggests that the authors are putting forward views so common as to be taken for granted as correct.

*

Sir Arthur Conan Doyle's *The White Company* (1891) demonstrates how the text constructs an ideological picture of political power and the ways in which the reader is drawn to accommodate it, if only temporarily. The setting of the book is France and England in the fourteenth century, and the story's context is the Black Prince's campaign to set Pedro the Cruel once more upon the throne of Spain. There is, however, much extraneous detail which shows aspects of life in medieval England and France. It is through this detail, and the authorial comments with which it is linked, that attitudes towards the distribution of power in both countries are transmitted.

How this happens can be explained by referring to a group of analagous texts: Ian Fleming's Bond novels. Although these belong to the genre of spy fiction and the first of them was written more than half a century after *The White Company*,[4] there are instructive similarities between the ways in which the ideology of the text operates. In *Bond and Beyond*,[5] Tony Bennett and Janet Woollacott describe how 'the mechanisms through which Bond is enlisted in the services of his country'[6] and, in particular, the way he is addressed in his official capacity as '007', 'inscribes him in the position of a subject bound by the requirements of duty'[7] through processes which, 'in specifying Bond's place and function in the world, also putatively stitch the reader into the subject positions produced by dominant ideologies of Englishness'.[8] Although the setting is so different, and the 'dominant ideologies' are as much concerned with class and power as with Englishness, the reader of *The White Company* is also stitched into ideologically charged subject positions.

Bennett and Woollacott point to the way in which Bond, before being given his mission, is constructed as a 'drifting subject . . . unsure of his position in the world and of his goal in life'.[9] Alleyne Edricson, the hero of *The White Company*, has similar uncertainties at the beginning of the novel. After years of identifying himself as a novice monk ('"But . . . it is surely true that I am already advanced several degrees in clerkship?"'(p.25)), he is reluctantly forced out into 'the world' by the terms of his father's will (p.24). Although the abbey is not a simple signifier, as was noted above in Chapter 2 (see p.26), its significance in relation to Alleyne is to have brought him up without knowledge of 'the world', so that he is both an educated man (his skills are detailed in the interview with the abbot and include painting, reading and geographical knowledge) and a kind of green child, observing the ways of his world with an innocent eye.

As such, when he meets with adventures on his journey from Beaulieu Abbey to his home in Minstead, he begins to note patterns and structures within the groups of people with whom he comes into contact, enabling the reader, by identification, to build up an image of English society in the fifteeenth century which makes evident the tensions within it, and to share his attitudes towards them.

Alleyne's attitudes, however, are only apparently those of an innocent, since he is aware that in going out into the world he must assume a new identity. Such an identity already awaits him: as a member of a family of 'good standing and repute', fit to marry into 'any family in the land' (p.292) he ranks by virtue of his birth and his brother's wealth amongst the nobility. On the other hand, the Socman of Minstead, his brother, is no Anglo-Norman, as the other nobles mentioned in the book are. Alleyne refers to himself and his brother as 'two boughs left upon this old Saxon trunk' (p.108), so that, like Scott's Wilfrid of Ivanhoe, they appear to be members of the old Saxon nobility. Although their links are in part with the feudal nobility, they are also associated with the commoners through their shared Saxon blood, and in fact before meeting his brother Alleyne hears news of him which makes him wonder if the Socman has made common cause with rebellious commoners and become 'the leader of a party against the State'. Alleyne's attitudes are thus in part those of an outsider, but also of a man who has a place within the social hierarchy, but an anomalous one, allowing him more flexibility in his responses to the people he meets.

In particular, an episode in which he intervenes to save an old woman from being beaten to death by a couple of robbers, and is himself set upon, gives a graphic picture of a breakdown of law and order and shows Alleyne both as respecting the law and as critical of it. Although he is thankful to be saved by the arrival of the bailiff of Southampton with a posse, he turns sick when the robbers are summarily executed. "'I am the law'", says the bailiff in extenuation; and the reader is left to draw unfavourable conclusions about a local state of anarchy which Conan Doyle later remarks could be found almost anywhere in England at that date (p.47).

These conclusions are confirmed by the unsympathetic picture given of the bailiff himself as fat, arrogant and superstitious, with little respect for the forms of law. There is a strong suggestion that he is a cause of the very crime he scourges so fiercely: he flaunts his wealth in rich and vulgarly bright velvets, and his corpulence speaks of greed. He is a man who invites envy: the outlaw who has stolen the old woman's red petticoat to wind around his head seems to be making a pathetic attempt to emulate the bailiff's rich purples and gold.

Bright clothing and jewels are a sign in *The White Company* not of a luxury to be enjoyed by proxy but of the self-indulgence of a ruling class which seems uninterested in its responsibility for the welfare of the commons. A number of Alleyne's adventures involve a confrontation between rebellious commoners and autocratic and disdainful nobles, and Alleyne's sympathies are divided between the parties. The incidents draw upon strongly condemnatory attitudes towards the representatives of the feudal state, a form of government which, however, as will be demonstrated later, is presented as firmly located in the past.

In at least one of these incidents, the jewels of the nobility are an exacerbating factor. This is the episode in which a runaway serf falls foul of the king's hunting party. The king is dressed in clothing which is rich and brilliant, if not best-suited to hunting, with 'silken tunic powdered with golden fleurs-de-lys', fur on his mantle and silver on his horse's harness (p.101). In his own way he is flaunting his wealth as much as the bailiff of Southampton does. He sees in the serf, not a human being under his care, but an anomaly: someone out of place who might consequently scare his game. The two men do not speak the same language; the serf speaks only English, the king, French. They stand therefore as representatives of alien groups, their lack of mutual understanding emphasized by the way in which the king, after rapping out his unintelligible question to the serf,

> thundered away, his knights lying low on their horses and galloping as hard as whip and spur would drive them . . . Away they drove down the long green glade . . . clad in every shade of velvet, fur or silk, with glint of brazen horn and flash of knife and spear.
>
> (p.102)

'Flash' is perhaps the most striking word here. Jewels and armour *flash*, and the king and his retinue *flash* through the glade. The hunting party, in rapid movement, seems to have no roots in the forest, unlike the static serf, who seems to have a natural right to be there. From a *legal* point of view, however, it is the king who has rights in the forest, whereas the serf, an outlaw, has not. The 'flash' of the royal party is opposed to the naturalness of the serf, rather as the repressed monks are opposed to the naturalness of Hordle John in the first episode. The serf, in fact, is associated firmly with natural objects: his sheepskin clothing is 'untanned' (p.99) and he is armed with no flashing steel but with a wooden cudgel. If anyone seems to have a right to be in the natural surroundings of the forest it is he; yet the legal rights (enforceable, as the king's interpreter Brocas makes clear, by savage penalties) belong to the 'artificial' nobles. This irony is reinforced by the impression of foreignness given by the king's French speech: the opposition is between France and England, nobles and commons, artificial display and plain, untreated and necessary clothing.

Faced with such an opposition, the direction of Alleyne's sympathies seems as though they must be with the English and natural party; but there are conflicting connotations in the phrases which describe king and serf which lead the reader to favour the ruling party after all. The serf is not wholly sympathetic: he is 'wild' and 'fierce' (p.102). So that if he represents nature it is an untamed nature which can be dangerous. Alleyne, who believes that the treatment meted out to the serf is fit 'to stir the blood and loose the tongue of the most peaceful', none the less is horrified by the 'unhallowed threats' which the serf shouts after the king's interpreter.

Similar associations surround the Socman, the serf's revolutionary leader. His description suggests the wild animal:

> The man turned upon him a face which was lion-like. . . . With his tangle of golden hair, his fierce blue eyes, and his large, well-marked features, he was the most comely man whom Alleyne had ever seen; and yet there was something so sinister and so fell in his expression child or beast might have shrunk from him . . . there was a mad sparkle in his eyes which spoke of a wild untamable nature.
>
> (p.106)

Animal associations surrounded the Saxon novice John of Hordle in the first episode of the novel, but they are a part of his attractiveness. If he is untamed, he is harmless and playful; his transgressions – drinking all the convent beer, upending the odious Brother Ambrose into the fishpond, or tricking a man into 'lending' him his clothes – are really practical jokes. Socman and serf suggest another side to Saxon naturalness and animalism – an aspect which is feral and dangerous.

What the two represent is a threat to the state; in particular, to the Lorings of Twynham Castle who hold their keep, ultimately, for the king. Later in the novel the threat is activated in a rebellion against the Lorings, which Lady Mary and Lady Maude Loring are able to put down by their bravery and the loyalty of their soldiers. There is no doubt in the description of this rebellion where the reader's sympathies should lie: the Lorings are sympathetic figures who have never done any harm to the commons.

In general, the portrayal of the nobility is not sympathetic, but they are none the less presented as natural rulers: the king, for instance, for all his alien qualities, is marked out by his appearance as a man with a natural right to rule, with his 'long finely-cut face and firm mouth' which 'marked the leader of men'(p.101). The nobility have a fineness of feature which seems to mark them out as a different species: Maude, for instance, has 'clear-cut composed features' (p.104). Differences between ruler and ruled are therefore unalterable, a part of the natural order.

It is among the upper classes, too, that patterns of good as well as bad government are to be found. In characters such as Sir Nigel Loring and the French leader du Guesclin, Conan Doyle shows how a ruling élite *ought* to behave: with consideration towards their inferiors, but maintaining firm discipline none the less. Such behaviour is linked to the kind of 'gentlemanly' qualities described in Chapter 3; it can also be attributed to a strong nineteenth-century tradition of nostalgia for the Middle Ages, which found in the values of feudal chivalry a pattern for the behaviour of the Victorian gentleman.

This tradition, as described by Marc Girouard in *The Return to Camelot*,[10] enforces on its adherents a duty to protect the poor and weak; and though Conan Doyle's picture of fifteenth-century society suggests that this duty was widely ignored in the chivalric period, there are enough upholders of the code – notably Sir Nigel – to suggest that the ideals of chivalry never entirely died out. Sir Nigel and his protégé, Alleyne, can be seen as natural governors of a prosperous society, acting not for themselves but in the light of ideals which promote universal welfare. The gentleman of the Victorian upper classes, avowedly motivated by the same ideals, then appears as their natural heir.

Thus, although there are times in the novel when Conan Doyle seems to be attacking the ruling élite, the answer to the abuses of feudalism is to be found in the actions of the governing class, not in any initiative of the commons. It is the duty of the nobility to become more responsible, not for the commons to take power into their own hands. The portrayal of revolt builds upon the images of wildness and bestiality which cluster around the discontented English commons to suggest strong condemnation. The strongest is reserved for a French revolt – though the responsibility for the rising is placed upon the feudal lord rather than upon the peasants who rise against him.

The episode in question, which forms a culmination to the theme of discontent and alienation which runs through the novel, centres around a rising of the Jacquerie as Alleyne and Sir Nigel Loring journey across France with their party to join the free company of mercenaries of which Sir Nigel has been made the leader.

At the castle of Sir Tristram de Villefranche, Sir Nigel notes with concern the half-starved condition of the peasants. From the conversation in the castle, it is clear that they have been driven to the point of revolt by Sir Tristram's exactions. Sir Tristram himself dismisses the commons as less than human: when his chaplain points out that his tenants have souls, Sir Tristram dissents vigorously. His wife complains about their ugliness: 'Ugly . . . without hair, without teeth, all twisted and bent'(p.335). It is cruelly foolish because it is Sir Tristram's own exactions which have made them so. But Sir Nigel, too, has shuddered at the appearance of the commons. Whatever the cause, there is something horrifying about them.

In the end it is the horror of their revenge which remains in the memory: a horror all the more ghastly because it falls on innocent and guilty alike. In the night the 'brushwood men' – the Jacquerie – rise against the castle and slaughter its inhabitants. Although the English party might have felt sympathetic to the peasantry while they are merely seen as victims of Sir Tristram, there is no suggestion of sympathy – even supposing the party had been detached enough from events to feel it – once the rising begins. The face of Sir Nigel's squire, Ford, amiable and chivalrous, hanging dreadfully distorted outside Alleyne's window is the key image of the revolt, since it is through seeing this that Alleyne becomes aware of what has been happening. Before the end of the fight, all within the castle, from the harsh Sir Tristram to his sympathetic chaplain, are dead, except for Sir Nigel and his immediate friends and followers. The message seems to be that revolt is dreadful and should be avoided; the way to necessary reform should be for the upper classes to change their ways, not for the lower classes to take matters into their own hands.

It is possible to sympathize with those who take part in rebellion, and Conan Doyle puts the case of the oppressed very strongly. Even Alleyne's friend, the likeable Hordle John, says that when the rights of the commons are ignored, 'it is time to buy arrow-heads'(p.94). Rebellion is the last resort to protect ordinary people against the oppression of an unfair social order, but in itself it is terrible, hurting friend and foe alike.

Even if rebellion is seen as a necesary evil, its contemporary relevance is doubtful. It has done its work: the English commons are free – 'the freest . . . in Europe'[11] – their liberties have been maintained, and contemporary revolt is unnecessary. Conan Doyle is a good example of those 'bourgeois humanists' Lukács describes in *The Historical Novel*:

> while they comprehend the necessity of revolutions in the past, and see in them the foundation for all that is reasonable and worthy of affirmation in the present, nevertheless they interpret future development in terms of a henceforth peaceful evolution on the basis of these achievements.[12]

Many of the attitudes expressed in *The White Company* can be found also in the work of other writers of the 1890s and 1900s. Even though many of the books show the individual acting heroically in a political cause, the effect is to suggest that government is best left to those most fitted to it by training and tradition. The most positive images are of systems of government which can be seen as progressing towards an impersonal bureaucratic state operated essentially by the upper and middle classes. The kind of government which the ordinary reader was used to was thus legitimated; despite its faults and disadvantages it was made to appear the fairest form possible in practice, and the end result of a long historical development.

*

The image of society presented by Stanley Weyman in his novels suggests a more advanced phase of this historical process than that shown by Conan Doyle, since Weyman's preferred periods were the sixteenth and seventeenth centuries, with some excursions into the early nineteenth. A clear line of evolution may none the less be traced between the fifteenth-century England of Conan Doyle and the sixteenth-century France of Weyman.

If Conan Doyle's heroes act according to the chivalric code as understood by the Victorians, with responsibilities as well as privileges, Weyman's are more likely to be the agents of a centralizing state, intent upon imposing justice and equality before the law. They have become servants of an impersonal force – agents of the evolutionary tendencies within society.

Weyman followed Scott in choosing for his settings moments of significant historical change. In many of his books, representatives of a new order confront the entrenched attitudes of men from a more primitive form of society. The stories end with the triumph of law and order and the building of a more stable society. The heroes have their part to play in this: they are shown to have earned their status through their ideals of disinterested service, and in fulfilling it they can be seen as acting as professionals, precursors of the bureaucrats who were becoming increasingly important in the government of late nineteenth-and early twentieth-century society.

The most extended description of what a good government might look like comes in *The Abbess of Vlaye* (1904). This is a romance set in the time of Henry IV of France. This king plays an important role in other books by Weyman – *A Gentleman of France* (1895) and *In the King's Byways* (1902). In many ways he is presented as an ideal monarch, for all his personal faults. He symbolizes in Weyman's work a caring, paternal authority: the seed of a 'modern' government in which every citizen's welfare counts.

In *The Abbess of Vlaye* Henry has just achieved power in France with the signing of the Edict of Nantes, but he is aware that in many parts of the country this is power in name only. Many of his people owe their allegiance to the great nobles in whose territory they live. These over-mighty subjects impose a rough justice, but the commons are harshly taxed so that the nobility can live in luxury. Because Weyman has chosen a moment of transition, which finds its focus in the events of the story, the new hegemony which is represented by Henry and his servants can be presented as both desirable in itself and as the shape of the future.

A popular rising in Périgord, the Crocan rebellion – in itself not so much a disease of the state as a symptom of a graver *malaise* – shows that matters are beginning to come to a head. The story concerns the efforts of the king's Lieutenant-Governor in Périgord, des Ageaux, to quell the rebellion and destroy the power of the man whose tyranny has provoked it, the Captain of Vlaye: a symbol of the power of the 'over-mighty subject'. This power is presented as the remnant of a more primitive type of government, to be replaced by one which can be seen as leading eventually to the early twentieth-century bourgeois state.

The first scene of the book, set in Henry's council chamber, functions both to explain the situation, and to introduce groups of characters who each represent a different aspect of government.

Most obviously sympathetic is Henry himself. Weyman has selected those elements from the historical Henry's 'myth' which show him as a man who cares less for personal power than for his country. At the head of the council table, he 'broods over his papers' knowing that he cannot answer his people's cry: 'Give us peace, give us law!' He will use men as tools if need be; but the men he chooses - des Ageaux in this book or de Marsac in *A Gentleman of France* – are chosen, not because of any charm of personality or wealth and position, but because they are utterly loyal, brave, and put their own interests second to his, which, of course, are those of France. Des Ageaux has no great fief from which to draw a power of his own; he is a member of the minor nobility and owes his advancement to Henry's patronage – as does the hero of *A Gentleman of France*. Such heroes seem, indeed, almost like emanations of Henry, as Weyman presents him; their ideals of service to their king and country mirroring the king's selfless care for his subjects' well-being.

Des Ageaux may not seem at first sight to resemble the king. He is dull and unromantic, indifferent to 'the favour of the ladies', with whom he is 'no favourite'. To men, 'he passed for a man more useful than most', which sounds competent but not dashing. He lacks the glamour of fine clothes and a splendid retinue: 'no man who ever came to court went with less splendour in the streets of Paris, or with a smaller following'(p.4). In the council described in the first chapter he appears as something of a Cinderella figure, placed 'near the bottom of the board'.

These negative qualities may seem surprising in a hero, but they have the effect of constructing des Ageaux as a neutral ground for qualities ('law' and 'justice') which seem not so much part of him personally but to be invested in him, abstractions which have their own existence and find in des Ageaux merely a temporal and local embodiment. He has more heroic qualities as well; he can fight, as evidenced by his appeal to 'the right of a soldier, who has fought for France'. He reveals an uncomplicated pride in doing his duty for his country. His most important attitude, however, is a love of justice which is 'part of his nature, part of his passion', and this is a major thread in the story.

Of all those present he is the most like the king. He 'featured Henry himself', both physically and mentally. Both care for their people in their own way. Des Ageaux's unglamorous lack of state comes partly from poverty (the king keeps him perennially short of money) but, more significantly, from a refusal to levy too high a tax on his region – or, presumably, to use the proceeds for himself.

The image of a pair of look-alikes, each a supporter of justice, at either end of the council table, gives the impression that law is made peripheral here, the central places being given to the irresponsible nobles. At the same time Henry and des Ageaux are in a strategic position: like a pair of pincers which could at any moment tighten and destroy the table. The positioning primarily emphasizes des Ageaux's lowly status and Henry's solitariness, but the possibility of their eventual victory is latent there.

Their sense of responsibility is not found among the great lords who make up the rest of the council. They 'whispered, or played tric-trac'; one has not even bothered to come, but has sent an agent instead, who speaks 'with thinly veiled impudence'. If des Ageaux is something of a Cinderella, so is Henry; but these two alone care for the people of France and suffer when 'the law was paralyzed, the great committed outrage, the poor suffered wrong'.

An opposition is thus set up at the beginning of the book, between Henry and des Ageaux on the one hand, and the great nobles on the other. If Henry and des Ageaux represent law, the nobles are not quite lawless. They keep order in their territory after a fashion: 'there is no finer wags [sic] in my country unless I will it', says the Constable, in what is no doubt intended to sound like sixteenth-century French. But they are responsible to no higher power, acting essentially in their own interests. They fear des Ageaux since he sets a standard of scrupulousness which could ruin them if it became generally enforced: 'And if he don't go, we shall have to mend our manners . . . and get our governments into order, too!' These nobles may be seen as belonging to an older world, laxer and more self-indulgent.

Typical is the Duke of Joyeuse, who follows des Ageaux on his mission, and provides a second centre of interest. He appears on the surface to be a more conventional romantic hero: a lapsed saint, a man whose preaching could fire a mob, and yet a womanizer. With his faintly dissolute appearance, 'pale with excess', his sense of personal honour, and his pride of race, he is clearly intended to appear intriguingly complex. His whims – following des Ageaux because he feels he has let him down by not supporting him at the council, plunging into the adventure on his own and in disguise, getting into a fight, and later endangering des Ageaux's whole enterprise, first by falling in love with the villainous Abbess of Vlaye

and then by saving a man whose life had been promised to the
revolutionary Crocans – are to some extent endearing, but potentially catastrophic. His individualism, as well as his glamour, makes
him a foil to des Ageaux, a man who will never put his own interests
first.

If one of the major functions of the council scene is to construct
the figure of des Ageaux, through his relationship with the good
King Henry and his opposition to the selfish power of the nobles, as
a representative of order and justice, the other is to set up the action
of the story through which the theme of law versus anarchy is
developed. Des Ageaux is given the task of settling the Crocan
rebellion and dealing with the man whose brutality had instigated it:
the master of the peasants, the Captain of Vlaye.

The picture of popular rebellion is very similar to that given in
The White Company: the Crocans are described with some sympathy, since it is plain that, like the Jacquerie in Conan Doyle's story,
they have been driven to desperation by harsh treatment. Their
appearance – ragged and deformed – is pitiable, but also frightening, giving the hostility they initially show towards des Ageaux an
almost animal quality. They lack discipline, which means that their
rebellion is unlikely to succeed against the powerful fighting ma-
chine of the Captain's mercenary force. Des Ageaux, with no
money to raise an effective force of his own, makes common cause
with the rebels to destroy the Captain, and has to provide his own
discipline before they can be of any military use to him. The
implication is not only that a discipline imposed from above is
necessary to make a rabble into an orderly society, but also that the
leaders who can impose it cannot be found amongst the populace.

In describing the alliance between des Ageaux and the Crocans,
Weyman makes it clear that his hero does not become a Crocan
himself. Des Ageaux imposes terms for his help: once the Captain is
destroyed, the peasants must return to their homes in peace, and
those who refuse to do so will be executed. Knowing that the rule of
law is best for the populace, des Ageaux imposes it from his own
position of power; his actions are contrasted with those of a re-
negade nobleman, Charles de Villeneuve, who has committed
himself to the Crocan cause without reserve. To throw in his lot with
the rebels is made to seem an aberration, motivated by personal
discontent and envy.

Charles would have accepted the sovereignty of the populace.
Des Ageaux insists that the populace accept his rule. In accepting

his terms, the Crocans tacitly give up the power they had implicitly claimed to be able to rule themselves (a power which their lack of discipline suggests they would have been incapable of wielding) and accept the sovereignty of the king and his servants. By implication, the accepted hierarchy is presented as 'natural' and right. Only the nobles are fitted to rule, but their authority must be regulated by the higher power of the king and used for the good of the people. Noblemen such as the Constable and the Duke of Joyeuse acknowledge neither true allegiance to the king nor responsibility for those in their care, and the result is the suffering and discontent which led to the rebellion. That this, rather than the popular discontent which is merely a symptom of misgovernment, is the true social evil against which Henry and his allies are struggling is clear from the fact that the villain of the book is no Crocan, but their oppressor, the Captain of Vlaye.

The Captain, des Ageaux's chief antagonist, is the most extreme example in the book of an individualistic and irresponsible nobility. Where the other nobles are corrupt, he is lawless; he extorts money from the peasants and treats them so brutally that they have revolted against all authority. He has (possibly) seduced Odette de Villeneuve, the Abbess of Vlaye, but he means to abduct and marry by force a much richer prize, the young Countess of Rochecouart. His bullying soldiers terrorize the family of a neighbouring nobleman, the Vicomte de Villeneuve, and try to trick and imprison the Duke of Joyeuse. He represents an extreme example of the individualism of Joyeuse and the other nobles. In him there is no acknowledgement of any authority other than his personal will, and the exercise of his power is solely in his own interest, not in any way on behalf of those who live under it. Because he is des Ageaux's opposite, the triumph of the 'impersonal' over the 'individualistic' is inscribed in his fall.

Once the Captain is dead, stabbed by des Ageaux's ally Joyeuse, des Ageaux is able to send the grateful Crocans home and begin to enforce the king's law. His immediate concern at the very end of the book is to raise Henry's flag as a sign of the re-establishment of royal power.

The image constructed by this final action resembles the famous image of the black soldier saluting the flag in Barthes' *Mythologies*.[13] As in the case of Barthes' photograph, a multiple significance can be teased out, drawing upon the cumulative significances of the events in the preceding story. The flag itself is a symbol of the king's power, replacing the anarchic petty tyranny of the Captain of Vlaye. A central power thus replaces the local; but if this seems to allow less freedom to the people, the impression is made to appear superficial. If the Crocan leaders, in allying with des Ageaux on his terms, have given up claims to a popular power, the king's power is augmented by what they have resigned, and it is exercised on their behalf. The flag is thus a symbol of government by consent, and can be seen as representing the people's will as much as that of the king.

Standing beneath the flag, des Ageaux is a symbol of the rule of law, of disinterested justice: his stance echoes another scene which confirms this. That is the scene in which he has a disobedient rebel hanged on a tree; a different kind of flag, but in its very harshness carrying the same symbolism: that des Ageaux will carry out what he threatens, and that his justice is impartial. The Crocans can thus be seen as justified in resigning power to him.

The new hegemony which des Ageaux represents is thus one which can be seen as constructed on behalf of the whole of society. It is an image of government which has something in common with the 'representative' democracy of the nineteenth and twentieth centuries: a first step, apparently, from 'personal' to 'impersonal'. This masks the fact that in reality power is vested, *not* in impersonal concepts of justice, but in a class: from the power of des Ageaux (a nobleman, but one without land, wealth or personal power of his own) to the bourgeois hegemony is a short step.

*

Weyman presents, perhaps, the most uncritical picture of a form of government which could be taken to be the logical precursor of a contemporary ideal. Other writers, such as Conan Doyle or Sabatini, whose books show them to have been more sympathetic to popular causes, might be expected to present a different picture. In fact, the attitudes towards state and society expressed in their books are much the same as Weyman's. In general, historical romances of this period (the last decade of the nineteenth and first of the twentieth century) are consistent in their political attitudes; a consistency particularly evident in their picture of popular movements.

Revolution is presented as the inevitable outcome of oppression and abuse of power, shown in the way that Conan Doyle's Sir Tristram simultaneously despises his tenants and tortures them to wring from them their pathetically small stock of coins, or in the way Weyman's Captain of Vlaye tyrannizes the Périgordian countryside. Even Baroness Orczy, normally far from showing any sympathy towards the revolutionaries, mentions at the beginning of *The Scarlet Pimpernel* (1905) that the French aristocrats had 'oppressed the people'.

The result of oppression is misery, deformity and savage resentment among the people. Weyman's Crocans are deformed; Conan Doyle's masterless serf is like a savage animal; and Orczy considers her mob of revolutionaries 'savage creatures' with 'vile passions'. The dominant image of revolution in all these authors is the mindless savagery of the mob and the corruptibility of the leaders. This is particularly true of books which, like Orczy's, use the French Revolution as a setting, and which contain strong echoes of attitudes to be found in Dickens's *A Tale of Two Cities* and the work of Carlyle.

In these books it is the image of the mob, driven by specific abuses by the aristocracy to rebellion and becoming in the process a mindless body, which is dominant; the ideology of rebellion is scarcely mentioned. Only in Rafael Sabatini's *The Trampling of the Lilies* (1906) is there a hint of it. This book opens with a picture of La Boulaye, the Marquis de Bellecour's secretary, wandering through the grounds of the Marquis's chateau in springtime:

> By the brook, plashing its glittering course through the park of Bellecour, wandered La Boulaye, his long, lean figure clad with a sombreness that was out of harmony in that sunlit, vernal landscape . . . . His face was pale and lean and thoughtful, but within his great intelligent eyes there shone a light of new-born happiness. Under his arm he carried a volume of the new philosophies which Rousseau had lately given to the world, and which was [*sic*] contributing so vastly to the mighty change that was impending.
>
> (p.9)

In one way this is a sympathetic portrait of the philosophy which in part inspired some of the revolutionaries. The book clutched under the secretary's arm seems almost a part of him: he is later (p.9) described as keeping it 'hugged' to his side. He himself is a sympathetic-sounding character, with his 'great intelligent eyes', and the feeling attaches itself to some extent to the book of which he takes such care.

There is another impression to counter this, however. La Boulaye's appearance is 'out of harmony' with the landscape, and his thinness and sombre dress sound a little sinister; an image of death in the middle of new growth. Rousseau's ideas are, moreover, qualified as 'metaphysical' and his book as 'musty' in comparison with the springtime landscape in which La Boulaye is walking. The implication is that there is something unnatural about such ideas: La Boulaye is out of tune with the natural scene and would be better occupied in something more suited to a young man in springtime – falling in love, perhaps. A moment later, confirming this implication, the heroine appears and Rousseau is – very properly, as Sabatini's approving comment makes clear – forgotten.

Rousseau's ideas are thus presented as over-academic ('musty'), with the implication that they cannot be realistic, and La Boulaye, in his concern with political philosophy, seems to be denying nature. Behind such an attitude lies an assumption that the proper concern of inexperienced young men is with the world of personal relationships, rather than with ideas about government which are dubious because they are based on theory rather than experience. There is even something ominous about the picture, as though the description of the secretary presages the deaths to come. At the same time, La Boulaye is not to be despised because of his admiration for Rousseau. It shows a proper concern for the good of humanity and makes the young secretary, with his 'great soul' (p.10), a far more worthy person than his master, the Marquis de Bellecour, whose savage treatment of the peasantry is symptomatic of the aristocratic abuses which inevitably drive the populace towards rebellion.

Sabatini presents specific episodes in *The Trampling of the Lilies* demonstrating these abuses, such as the apparent beating to death of the secretary by the orders of the Marquis (p.32), and his attempt to enforce the *droit de seigneur* on the daughter of one of his tenants (p.25). At this point in the story the reader's sympathies must lie with La Boulaye, despite any doubts about his political theories, since he nearly loses his life for declaring honourable love to the Marquis de Bellecour's daughter.

Even La Boulaye's friend Robespierre is more sympathetic than the Marquis; after the flogging of the secretary, when, through the heroine's agency, La Boulaye has been saved from being actually killed, Robespierre, an acquaintance of La Boulaye's friend and teacher Duhamel, comes upon him trying to revive the young man. The revolutionary's 'weak, kindly eyes'(p.38) grow angry, and his mouth, notable for its 'sensitiveness', curls. He offers to save the young man by taking him off in his carriage and tending him – an offer of some generosity, as Duhamel's grateful reaction makes clear. It is the beginning of a relationship whose intimacy suggests that Robespierre is far from being the evil monster that Orczy makes of him in *The Triumph of the Scarlet Pimpernel*, since La Boulaye, though unworldly, is sound enough in his choice of people to love, as his feelings for both Duhamel and Suzanne de Bellecour attest. On the other hand, Robespierre is wearing garments as 'sombre' as those of La Boulaye, and he shares La Boulaye's spareness; his lips may be sensitive but they are also thin; he is 'singularly pale', and there is about him a 'contradiction' which, like the skeletal suggestions of the figure of La Boulaye, have ominous as well as pleasing associations (p.38). Yet Robespierre's horror about what has happened is far more humane than the reactions of the Marquis's friends.

One in particular, the Viscount d'Ombréville, shows attitudes as despicable as those of Conan Doyle's Sir Tristram. He is betrothed to Suzanne de Bellecour, and, during the Terror, is arrested and imprisoned. Suzanne pleads for his life with La Boulaye, who, as a friend of Robespierre and a popular leader who has been involved in the Revolution since its beginning, is now a Deputy and a man of influence. It is not an influence sufficient to save d'Ombréville, so, Sidney Carton-like, La Boulaye engineers d'Ombréville's escape and is arrested in his turn for abetting an aristocrat, submitting to imprisonment and probable death because he believes Suzanne genuinely loves d'Ombréville.

Suzanne, however, is shocked at the exchange, and takes it for granted that d'Ombréville will give himself up to save La Boulaye. She is horrified to find, however, that d'Ombréville does not consider that 'honour' applies to relations between nobility and the populace: '"You have thought that it was perhaps my duty as a man of honour to go and effect the rescue of this fellow . . . were he a gentleman . . . I should not have hesitated . . . but this *canaille!*'"(p.218). True and false ideas of honour and what constitutes a gentleman are in question here, much as they are in some of Weyman's books, such as *Under the Red Robe* (1894) or *A Gentleman of France* (1893). This whole issue is connected with the idea of 'Englishness', and will be discussed in more detail in Chapter 5. What is immediately clear, however, is that d'Ombréville's attitudes towards the populace are substantially those of Sir Tristram de

Villeneuve towards his peasants in Conan Doyle's *The White Company*, denying them true humanity and stressing their animality.

On the other hand, when the victims rise in revolt, they are not presented primarily as victims. They are objects of horror and fear. Physical malformation reflects an inner monstrosity. The mob who storm the château of the Marquis de Bellecour are certainly as savage as Weyman's Crocans, and the representatives of the revolutionary army who appear later in the story not only lack discipline quite as much as Weyman's Crocan camp does, but are little better than a collection of highway robbers.

The picture of the mob who attack de Bellecour's castle appears to have been based on the picture of revolution by Delacroix, *Liberty Guiding the People*: the women who stream into the courtyard side by side with the men wear the 'crimson caps' of the Jacobin, 'their bosoms bare' (p.50). If in Delacroix's painting a bare bosom signified the nurturing qualities of Liberty, and the fearlessness and love of freedom which cast aside the conventional bonds of modesty, in Sabatini's description it suggests rather the immodesty of those beside themselves with a maenad savagery; they are part of a 'fierce, unkempt band' (p.50) and men and women alike are 'howling and roaring like the beasts of prey they were become' (p.56).

The animal imagery is reminiscent of Conan Doyle's peasant revolutionaries. In this book it sits oddly with the later presentation of d'Ombréville's attitudes: the reader is expected to deprecate d'Ombréville's condemnation of a peasant as '*canaille*', but to identify with the same attitude in this scene. Certainly the condemnation of the mob, as a symptom of rebellion, is strong; not only are its members dehumanized, but the song which symbolizes the Revolution is damned – as they sing the *Marseillaise*, a 'fearful chorus', the peasants sound like the 'choirs of hell' (p.50). In the face of the mob, the aristocrats recover a little of the reader's esteem by their bravery whereas the mob turns tail as soon as the soldiers come.

The mob of Bellecourt is presented as part of a general unleashing of mob violence during the Revolution; the National Convention is said to have motives of its own for letting the mobs 'butcher' aristocrats (p.60), as though its members were not themselves moved either by the consciousness of a 'long-standing debt of hate' (p.56), like the mobs, or by La Boulaye's idealism, but taking part in an unscrupulous power game.

The implication that men of ideals and mindless mobs alike are manipulated by unscrupulous power-seekers is another traditional image of revolution which is clearly expressed in the romances. It is again familiar from Dickens; this is very much the picture of the manipulated mob shown in *Barnaby Rudge* (1841), which goes further in presenting the mob as monstrous than Sabatini's book does. In both books mob violence is terrible to no purpose; it is not the mob's members who will gain any profit to be had from revolution. This does not lead the reader's sympathies towards the populace, however; if they allow themselves to be manipulated for the benefit of others, it is because they are too stupid to realize the way they are being used and, in any case, left to themselves they could achieve nothing at all, since they lack the discipline necessary for purposeful action. In itself this aspect suggests the falsity of revolutionary ideals such as liberty and equality: ordinary men and women need to be led, which presupposes a need for a class of leaders.

What happens to the revolutionaries in *The Trampling of the Lilies* when they become leaderless illustrates this. When Suzanne de Bellecour tries to escape from France in the aftermath of the attack on her father's château, she is captured by a company of the revolutionary army. They have become detached from the main army, and their captain, Charlot Tardivet, is missing. Charlot has encouraged them to become little better than highway robbers, looting from the aristocrats they arrest and living off what they can wrest from the local peasantry. Without Charlot, they find nothing better to do than to sit about aimlessly and get drunk – too drunk to guard Suzanne properly. In fact, they become, in Sabatini's words, 'a human chaos' (p.81). Charlot, for all his faults, is a leader who can make them into some kind of a force, even if its aim is merely extortion. They respect him for his mixture of heroism and brutality, even when the brutality is directed at them: when he 'barked out a sharp word of command', they shout '*Vive le Capitaine Charlot!*' (p.82).

The soldiers are like the outlaw black in Conan Doyle's *The White Company* (1891), who in his desire for a bit of finery ties an old woman's red petticoat around his head; the glittering appearance of the bailiff of Southampton who is following him makes it clear that the conspicuous expenditure of the wealthy leads to the longing for such fripperies which has driven the outlaw to crime. The soldiers have added to their uniform all sorts of odd scraps of aristocratic finery: a 'coat of yellow brocaded silk', or a 'three-cornered red hat, richly laced in gold' (p.77). But these are no more natural to them than the petticoat on the outlaw's head: they cannot keep them in proper condition, and the coat is stained with oil and wine, and torn.If the reader can have a little sympathy for the rags of the revolutionary mob when they are contrasted with the 'elegant, bejewelled, bepowdered' aristocrats (p.50), there is a strong implication in the description of the soldiers that the aristocrats, as lawful owners of the finery, somehow deserve it because they can make sure it is kept clean, whereas the soldiers do not. The bedraggled state of their brocades is also symptomatic of their inability to rule themselves; their lack of any discipline and need for a leader, however contemptible, is reminiscent of Weyman's Crocans, who needed the firm leadership of des Ageaux before they could become a fighting force.

Left to themselves, the populace can act to no purpose; manipulated by a bad leader, who plays on their grievances, they are worse than this and become an inhuman mob. It is the picture which had survived from the fiction of Dickens – (for example, *Barnaby Rudge* (1841), or *A Tale of Two Cities* (1859) – or Matthew Arnold's concern about the riotous potential of a too-free populace.[14]

The Trampling of the Lilies gives a bleak picture of a political situation in which the natural leaders have abrogated their responsibilities and those who have seized power in their turn are totally unfitted to rule. Rebellion is portrayed as a kind of boil on the body of a healthy society; a sore which has come to a head. The nature of a healthy society is not discussed. Sabatini does not resolve the political situation in his book by suggesting a hopeful outcome, but simply removes his hero and heroine from it, to make a new life for themselves outside France. Logically, however, a state which avoided the abuses described in the novel would be one not unlike that prefigured in *The Abbess of Vlaye*, in which the king was beginning to provide a strong centralized government, carried out by his servants who were personally disinterested and cared only for ruling the people, on their own behalf, with a necessary firmness. Such servants are men like des Ageaux in *The Abbess of Vlaye*, Alleyne in *The White Company*, who feels a mixture of horror and sympathy at the resentful defiance of the masterless serf, or La Boulaye in *The Trampling of the Lilies* with his 'great soul'. It is these figures and others like them who stand for good government in the romances, and their similarity is echoed by an agreement in picturing the causes of disruption and anarchy.

*

The historical romances of this period can be read both as a warning of what might happen when a 'natural' ruling order neglected its responsibilities and as praise for the kind of government the readers themselves were accustomed to, even if, as in *The Abbess of Vlaye*, this co-existed with a sense of nostalgia for a more individualistic society. It was an image which was very closely involved with two others: that of 'Englishness' (it is noticeable that when an 'unhealthy' society is portrayed the setting is likely to be France), and that of a 'natural' social hierarchy. These two topics will be treated at more length in the following chapters.

Chapter 5

English heritage

The semi-public body which now takes care of our ancient buildings has taken the name of 'English Heritage'. It is an evocative title, suggesting a peculiar national virtue handed down to us through countless generations. The associations are themselves ancient ones; they evoke a mixture of nostalgia and pride which has been used often enough in the past to help create a sense of national identity. That such an identity can be built from feelings which exclude a large part of the nation suggests how confusedly and uncritically they are held; this particular blend of emotion is in itself a myth, and one of peculiar potency.

Almost all the older authors who have been considered so far called upon this sense of identity at some time or another in their career – oddly, since few of them actually were English. Weyman, who used it least in its most explicit form, was English, but in the latter part of his career he settled in Wales. Conan Doyle was from an Irish family but spent his early years in Scotland. Orczy was Hungarian; Sabatini, an Anglo-Italian who was born in Italy. Even Heyer's family were of German origin. So the national myth can be constructed by anyone; it is simply a matter of using the right materials.

In Chapter 4 it was argued that the political values implicit in the historical romances of the 1890s and 1900s were favourable to a state which remained firmly in the hands of 'natural' leaders from the upper or upper-middle classes. These political values, incorporated into the descriptions of characters and the *semes* which surround them, are closely associated with images of 'the gentleman' and of 'Englishness' which help to support each other. In this chapter I should like to explore ways in which the 'Englishness' presented in the work of Conan Doyle, Stanley Weyman, Baroness Orczy,

Rafael Sabatini and Jeffrey Farnol supports a favourable image of the English state as free and democratic, yet firmly led, to the benefit of all, by the upper and upper-middle classes. Feminine historical romance of the kind initiated by Georgette Heyer is not likely to show links of this kind, yet I should like to argue that this too draws upon the concept of 'Englishness' and that this became one aspect of the female construction of the romantic hero.

Of these writers, Conan Doyle and Weyman were both writing in the 1890s. Orczy and Sabatini began their writing careers in the 1900s, but both were still writing during the 1920s, and the book by Sabatini most relevant to this chapter was published in 1925. Farnol published his first novel, *The Broad Highway*, in 1910, and Georgette Heyer published *her* first book in 1921. The works discussed thus come from four decades, and it might be expected that they would show changes which match the changes in society over this period. To a certain extent they do: Farnol's image of Englishness is more domestic and rural than Conan Doyle's, for instance, and Heyer's use of the concept is different in function from those of the other writers. What is more striking is the degree of continuity, both in the image and its function.

'Englishness' is not specific to historical romance, of course; rather, it is a structure of feeling disseminated through a wide variety of media, from literature and painting to the teaching of subject disciplines in schools, or attitudes towards leisure and the countryside. Nor is supporting the political status quo its only significance. Claud Cockburn has suggested that the combination of 'Englishness' and fighting is part of the escapist pleasure of the early texts.[1] Readers in the 1900s – he was thinking of those who read Jeffrey Farnol's *The Broad Highway* in 1910 – turned to such books to relieve the stress of real fears, at a time when international tension was growing. For the moment they could feel that warfare was a pasteboard, illusory affair, nothing to be afraid of; while, at a deeper level, their faith that their country deserved their loyalty was reaffirmed.

It may be, however, that the original function of national sentiment was more concerned with smoothing over the divisions within society than with England's position in the world. Stuart Hall *et al.* have described a contemporary version of this national image in *Policing the Crisis* as 'an extremely powerful cluster of patriotic sentiments', important because it helps to confirm commitment to British institutions (or, at least, to the 'vague image' which represents them in the popular mind), and to suggest a unity of interest, which in the last resort, binds all classes together.[2] The image includes such characteristics as facing reality, use of practical, commonsense viewpoints, tolerance and moderation. It has the function of locating popular feeling in the area which Marx defined as 'Social Democracy', which, he wrote, is 'epitomised in the fact that democratic-republican institutions are demanded as a means, not of doing away with two extremes, capital and wage labour, but of weakening their antagonism and transforming it into a harmony'.[3] The 'national image' created by the texts combined with the images of state and society to give a view of Engish society as essentially harmonious and sound.

Philip Dodd has remarked upon the way in which a concept of 'Englishness', which was sited in such institutions as the public schools and the universities of Oxford and Cambridge and associated with a positive valuation of 'manliness', was 'reconstituted' (since this was one form of an enduring concept which was constantly being remade) in the late nineteenth century.[4] This was not a matter of a dominant group imposing an identity upon a subordinate one; none the less Dodd considers that 'there is certainly evidence to support the thesis that Englishness and the national culture were reconstituted *in order* to incorporate and neuter various social groups – for example, the working class, women, the Irish – who threatened the dominant social order'.[5]

The question of how such groups could be led to accept a national identity which seemed to exclude them may be resolved by their seeing the concept in a framework of a functionalist society; the organic analogy which formed the base of Herbert Spencer's social theory was a popular image and one which allowed each social group its own function deriving from its peculiar character. Philip Dodd quotes J. A. Hobson's *The Crisis of Liberalism: New Issues of Democracy* (1909) to illustrate this: while 'Each limb, each cell has a "right" to its due supply of blood', each 'contributes to the life of the organism according to its powers'.[6] Classes excluded from the concept of 'Englishness' were portrayed as each in their own way essential to its maintenance: women as 'a superior race, forced to operate on a lower level' in Elaine Showalter's words;[7] the working class 'construed predominantly in terms of their (manual) labour'.[8] and the Celtic nations of the British Isles as belonging to the past, and therefore more 'primitive', closer to nature and the ways of our ancestors, than was 'metropolitan England'.[9] Thus the dominant group retained its superiority while the subordinate groups were incorporated because in some ways the stereotyped image which defined them was flattering, even if at the same time it was a marginalizing one.

Other reasons for accepting an excluding national image are suggested by Patrick Wright, and are particularly relevant to historical romance. He argues that:

> it is characteristic of dominant particularism to permeate the fabric of social life as if it were a universal legitimising principle in itself – the bourgeois-imperial sense of national identity and belonging is often projected as the absolute essence of a social life which it also places conveniently beyond question.[10]

A view of national identity which is seen from the standpoint of the bourgeoisie is put forward as 'natural', and this is persuasive enough to draw other groups in, for the moment, to share it. The sense of an identity, of belonging, is attractive at a time of rapid social transformation because the 'traditional hierarchy of socially binding values is eroded' and the 'everyday "sense of historical existence" becomes progressively anxious, searching more intently for answers which – in the dislocated experience of modernity – seem to be less readily forthcoming'.[11]

Modern British society thus creates a need for a sense of identity which reaches back to a past in which society was linked by binding values: a 'rural idyll' of 'deep England' and a 'National Heritage' seen in terms of the survival of places and objects invested with an aura of tradition, such as Mentmore Towers or Calke Abbey.[12] Though the way of life at Mentmore, as described by someone who remembered it 'at its peak',[13] may seem far removed from the everyday experience of ordinary men or women, it could seem worthy of preservation as part of a 'golden' past: one, moreover, when Britain was affluent as well as stable, and an important power in the world.

Hall *et al.* connect the 'external aspect' of 'Englishness' with imperialism and consider that it influences reaction to all foreigners and immigrants: a belief that 'the English possessed special qualities as a people which protected them from military defeat' which was 'grounded in the Empire, backed by military, naval and economic supremacy'. Foreigners are seen as lacking 'just that combination of qualities which make the English what they are':[14] a view which gives a sense of superiority towards, for instance, 'immigrant labour' and helps to make the English working class a 'bourgeois proletariat'. These were sentiments which Hall *et al.* saw as operative in the 1970s.

However, this particular national sentiment also predates the international tensions which led to the World Wars. Marc Girouard[15] associates it with the concept of chivalry and the qualities of a gentleman. The Victorian chivalric ideal to which he refers puts a high value on such qualities as generosity, care for dependants and the weak (such as women), loyalty, and an unassuming bravery which is all the more real for being understated.

It is easy to see why the Victorian gentry liked to see themselves as holding such values; they are the reverse of the hard-nosed competitiveness which had come to be associated with industrialism in the early part of the nineteenth century. The concept of chivalry was part of the post-Romantic tradition which rejected such competitive attitudes. Hence its power: Girouard gives examples of this image of gentlemanly behaviour drawn not only from novels but from the diversions and familiar letters of the period.

Many men from the English upper and middle classes believed they held such values in reality and this gave them a feeling of conscious superiority in comparison with men from other nations. Commenting on reports of the last hours of the *Titanic*, Girouard writes: 'The almost unanimous tendency of Anglo-Saxon witnesses to assume that anyone who behaved badly was an Italian or some other form of foreigner needs to be treated with caution.'[16] To be 'Anglo-Saxon' stood for something, it seems: decent behaviour was assumed to be a natural part of it.

Among the writers who came to prominence in the 1890s it is Conan Doyle who expresses such feelings most clearly. In his work, national feeling, respect for the fighting man, and chivalric ideals combined to provide an image of behaviour that readers might respect, and which could mask the realities of power and inequality of which Conan Doyle himself seems to have been uneasily conscious. At the same time, he was anxious to propagate the idea that England's interests needed to be protected against those of new industrial powers, in particular those of Germany; so that the national myth may be said to have a dual role in his work.

The White Company (1899) is set in the context of the Black Prince's campaigns in Aquitaine, in particular that on behalf of the claimant to the Spanish throne, Pedro the Cruel. In this book the English are presented as pre-eminent fighters. Even the French knight du Guesclin, no friend to the English, admires their fighting skills: he admires them as soldiers and as upholders of chivalric values. He will fight against 'a true Englishman' but not against one of the Gascon lords who fight under the English banner. (It goes without saying that such a fight would be considered a treat and an honour.) The effect is to suggest that, though other nations (such as the French) may contain a few chivalrous knights like du Guesclin himself, the true home of chivalry is in England.

Certainly, both Gascons and foreign princes show up badly beside the English at the Black Prince's court. The Gascons are 'chaffering for terms like so many hucksters'. The King of Navarre wants to delay fulfilling his commitment to Prince Edward: '"He sets his kingdom up to the highest bidder"', comments the Prince (p.218). The derisive 'huckster' is a reminder that trade is ungentlemanly, and therefore unchivalrous: is this more compensatory denigration?

If the French, or nearly French, have the souls of traders, the representatives of other nations are worse. Don Pedro, the Spanish pretender, would be a liability at any court. He takes advantage of the Prince's generosity and politeness to borrow more and more money from him. Despite the Prince's objection that '"things are not ordered this way in Aquitaine"', he insists on sending for any girl who takes his fancy, rather as one might send for sandwiches or a bottle of beer (p.255).

When the Prince objects, Pedro thinks him mean: he would not be so grudging a host. Respect for women and monogamy is something such a foreigner cannot understand. The spread of such chivalric attitudes, with their associations with Victorian family life, can presumably be seen as an advantage to outweigh the wasting of the land and the dubious value of a campaign aimed at restoring the appalling Pedro to his hapless people.

War seems, in fact, to be valuable for its own sake, an attitude which fits in with the strongly nationalistic, even chauvinist, attitude characteristic of Conan Doyle's 'medieval' fiction, and may to some extent explain its popularity. All the positive virtues attributable to soldiers are associated naturally with the English, who 'flew to their arms as to their birthright'.

War indeed is England's 'trade', 'her exports archers and her imports prisoners', and to feel that the English have been successful in it might well have been tempting when other forms of trade had come to seem less naturally their 'birthright' than formerly.

Certainly there is no suggestion that other kinds of trade might have been preferable. Rather, the marches of Picardy and Normandy having been laid to waste, the notion of breaking through to new territory (and wasting that, presumably) 'was a golden prospect for a race of warriors'.

For Conan Doyle, therefore, English virtues were bound up with the warlike prowess of the knights and, even more (because they are presented as pure Saxon rather than as Anglo-Norman), the English yeomanry and peasants who were represented by the archers and men-at-arms of the White Company. Conan Doyle's picture of English society was confirmed by the popular history of the period. In the 1870s John Richard Green's *A Short History of the English People* (1874) was a book whose popularity – a popularity which rested to a large extent on the picture of Englishness it presented – was attested by Sir Arthur Quiller-Couch, who, speaking at Cambridge in 1916 of 'the shock of awed surprise which fell upon young minds presented, in the late 'seventies or early 'eighties of the last century with . . . Green's *Short History of the English People*', explained that its readers found 'our ancestry . . . radiantly legitimized'.[17] Although Green was dead by the time Conan Doyle brought out his first book, *Micah Clarke* (1889), it is highly improbable that so indefatigable a researcher should have been unaware of his work.

Green draws a picture of the English as being primarily a body of freemen, each with a say in the running of village affairs, with an 'eorl' or 'aetheling' to lead them whose 'claim to precedence rested simply on the free recognition of his fellow villagers'.[18] But 'it was the freeman who was the base of village society', and 'within the township every freeman or ceorl was equal'.[19] The Anglo-Saxons came from a background of Germanic culture and custom, according to which the voice of every freeman counted in the village moot.

This is 'the groundwork of English history', the place where 'England learned to be a "mother of Parliaments"'.[20] Its essence is 'the strife and judgement of men giving freely of their own reed and setting it as freely aside for what they learn to be the wiser reed of other men' through persuasion, 'the one force which can sway freemen to deeds such as those which have made England what she is'. Although, like Conan Doyle, Green stresses the warlike qualities of the English ('a grim joy in hard fighting was already a characteristic of the race'), they are tempered by a respect for others which seems to suggest that warfare is not entered into lightly.

Individual freedom, the right of the ordinary person to have his say, equality modified only by the existence of an aristocracy which governs by the consent of the people: these are the essentials of Green's picture of Anglo-Saxon society, and the implication of a phrase such as 'the groundwork of English history' is that they continue to be essential characteristics. Conan Doyle wrote of a period when this 'groundwork' was far back in the past, but it can be seen that his fourteenth-century Englishmen are the products of a society which has not radically changed its values.

Thus, when Sir Tristram de Villefranche in the *The White Company* speaks slightingly of the French peasantry ('"If you pummel Jacques Bonhomme he will pat you"', p.334), Sir Nigel thinks of Samkin Aylward and Hordle John: 'he who pummelled them would come by such a pat as he would be likely to remember'. This suggests that he not only finds Sir Tristram's statement absurd, but is also respectful of the independent spirit of his followers, which to Sir Tristram is 'the insolence of the base-born'. Sir Tristram is incapable of appreciating the relationship between Sir Nigel and his companions, who are friends as much as they are servants, and indeed finds Sir Nigel's attitude 'contemptible'. Samkin and John are never afraid of speaking their minds. They prize their liberties, protected by 'charters, liberties, franchises, usuages, privileges, customs and the like'. John indicates that he would fight to protect them (p.94).

The long list of legal protections, with quaint-sounding terms ('usuages'), suggests the development through time of a system which grew up haphazardly and piecemeal, but is none the less strong. It is case-law rather than code, and is just the kind of system which could be predicted as arising from the 'moots' Green had described, with 'reed' given on a multitude of specific instances as they arose: judgements which then became precedents because they could be accepted as right (through 'persuasion') according to the dictates of a characteristically English 'common sense'.[21]

The system is shown by Green as having grown from the bottom up, and Hordle John's pride in its results suggests that Conan Doyle is implying this too. Confrontation between populace and aristocracy might wreck such a system and lead to the imposition of a constitution and a code of justice which – like the French Napoleonic Code, perhaps – might be theoretically more sound but which would not work so well in practice, or so much to the benefit of the people. It is a feeling still operative in twentieth-century

Britain, evident in British distaste for a written constitution, or the sentiments expressed by Mrs Thatcher in her 'Bruges speech' of 1990, and it has important social implications, inhibiting confrontation and justifying consensus.

The concurrence of the English aristocracy is suggested in *The White Company* by Sir Nigel's respect for John and Samkin. Green had stated that the power of the leader in English society was based on 'the free recognition of his fellow villagers'. In the days of which Conan Doyle wrote, such an ideal situation had long passed away. Conan Doyle's image of medieval society implies that a Norman aristrocracy had tried to impose foreign values on the native English society: an implication everywhere present, in the disaffection of the serf Brocas (p.100), for instance, and the lack of understanding shown by the king.

If the general breakdown in law and order, noted by Alleyne on his journey from Beaulieu, and the discontent which led to the Socman's rebellion are in part shown as due to the insensitivity of the 'foreign' aristocracy, the situation and character of the minor nobility (such as Sir Nigel, with his respect for John and Samkin) give hope for the stability of English society in the future. Sir Nigel is becoming assimilated into the English social system, which in its turn is changing to accommodate the new aristocracy. The Socman of Minstead may lead a revolt against the Norman power which the Lorings represent, but his heir is Alleyne Edricsson,who has been brought up in the Anglo-Norman monastery and who becomes Sir Nigel's squire and disciple. Alleyne's mind is no longer purely Saxon, though he can sympathize with Brocas when he swears at the king and feel that royalty and nobility are alike to blame for the serf's state of mind. Eventually, he will inherit Sir Nigel's position as well as some of his values, through his marriage to Nigel's daughter.

Saxon democracy and freedom can be seen as conquering the conquerors, but in the process they are tempered with some of the more positive values of the aristocrats: which, in *The White Company*, means the virtues of chivalry. The English heritage in Conan Doyle's work is not simply what has been handed down from 'Saxon forefathers' but an assimilative tendency which has the power of taking the best of foreign values and drawing them into the formation of national society. Although the work of both Green and Conan Doyle has a certain egalitarian tendency, the impression given is that democracy is something already achieved in English society. In a sense it was always there. Threats are dealt with by accommodating whatever is positive in new systems and values. A stable society has grown up in a natural way by a continual process of concession which leaves its essential character unchanged, the result of a consensus of free minds.

*

The association of Englishness with freedom and democracy is particularly striking in Conan Doyle but is to a degree typical of historical romance in general. Almost all Conan Doyle's younger contemporaries[22] give some picture of English superiority – in war if need be, since English values are worth fighting for – linked to a positive image of English government and society.

Although Weyman does not use the patriotic theme overtly, since he sets so few of his novels in England, he constructs a group identity very similar to that of Conan Doyle's English characters for the Huguenots in his French stories, who as Protestants could be thought of as nearer than other Frenchmen to English values. The natural gentlemanliness of the Marquis de la Rochefoucauld in *Count Hannibal* and of de Marsac in *A Gentleman of France* is reminiscent of the qualities of Sir Nigel and Alleyne, and gentlemanliness is a central theme explored in *Under the Red Robe*. But a sense of Englishness much closer to that shown by Conan Doyle can be found in the works of Baroness Orczy, Jeffrey Farnol and to a lesser extent Rafael Sabatini.

The denigratory portrait of revolution given in Baroness Orczy's *The Scarlet Pimpernel* (1905) has already been described(see p.58). This writer's picture of 'Englishness' is close in many ways to that given by Conan Doyle. At the same time, *The Scarlet Pimpernel* shows her to be drawing on other strands of Englishness: in particular, on the concept of 'deep England' which is more fully developed in the work of Jeffrey Farnol, whose *The Broad Highway* was published only five years after *The Scarlet Pimpernel*. This does not mean that Orczy was an innovator: something of the 'deep England' feeling can be found in the work of A. E. W. Mason in the 1890s, and in any case Orczy herself was not a writer who showed herself readily adaptable to changes in the public mood. The attitudes expressed in *The Scarlet Pimpernel* can be found in sequels published as late as the 1920s such as *The Triumph of the Scarlet Pimpernel* (1922) and *The Adventures of the Scarlet Pimpernel* (1929).

There can be no doubt about the strength of the opposition between French democrats and English aristocrats in her work, or where the author's sympathies lie. Revolutionary Frenchmen in *The Scarlet Pimpernel* and its sequels are portrayed as loathsome: selfish, greedy, boastful, rude and treacherous. To the Paris mob, killing has become a pastime: in *The Triumph of the Scarlet Pimpernel* the very children clutch little images of the guillotine. *The Adventures of the Scarlet Pimpernel* (1929) contains a number of stories which show revolutionaries acting out of personal spite rather than from ideals. The leaders of the revolution, in particular, are monstrous, power-hungry creatures; Robespierre is cowardly as well.

Even the best of the French, though, have their failings. Suzanne de Tournay in *The Scarlet Pimpernel* is charming, but her mother is 'the very personification of unbending pride' and her brother is a 'little bantam', ridiculous in his touchy sense of honour. French royalists, like the Baron de Batz in *Eldorado*, can be self-seeking and unscrupulous. Also, however perfunctorily the case for the revolutionaries may be presented, the Revolution can be seen as arising from a diseased society where the gulf between aristocracy and populace had become too wide – the fruition of tendencies which Conan Doyle had portrayed in medieval France.

The image of Britain, on the other hand, is a very positive, almost self-congratulatory one. Few lower-class characters are represented, and the landlord and clientele of the Fisherman's Rest, the inn which the League of the Scarlet Pimpernel use as a safe house when setting off for their expeditions, may stand for all. They are portrayed as a little stupid, fond of voicing their opinions, but full of individuality, self-respecting and comfortable in a free country.

Their very diet is better: honest bread and cheese instead of potatoes and pickled herring, which Orczy notes as poor fare for the Paris revolutionaries in *The Triumph of the Scarlet Pimpernel*. English habits are cleaner, too. Both Orczy and Sabatini put a high value on personal cleanliness, going some way towards suggesting that dirt is a lower-class characteristic. Dirt and cleanliness have their nationalist aspects, too. In *The Triumph of the Scarlet Pimpernel*, the unclean tables of the 'fraternal supper' compare ill with the immaculate sanded floors of the Fisherman's Rest; in *The Scarlet Pimpernel*, the Calais tavern where Chauvelin awaits the Pimpernel is by contrast 'horribly squalid', its walls 'stained with varied filth'.

The landlord shows his status as a 'freeborn citizen' by smoking in the face of his guests, in contrast to Jellyband of the Fisherman's Rest, who may be 'eager, alert and fussy' as he greets Lord Anthony Dewhurst, but is quite ready to talk to him on equal terms without forced insolence. The English working classes know their place - Jellyband's friend Mr Hempseed 'respectfully touches his forelock' – but they are not oppressed by the English aristocrats, who are, in fact, ready to chat with them, compliment their cooking and ask after their orchards.

Lord Tony Dewhurst, Sir Percy's lieutenant, is 'a very perfect type' of such aristocrats: lively and courteous, if not very clever, he is 'a good sportsman' and makes himself a favourite with all classes of people. It is this typical Englishman whom Sir Percy is aping: the more easily since in many ways he *is* one. He has the sportsmanship and easy manners, the bravery and instinctive chivalry. What he lacks is the stupidity he assumes.

As for the English government, it is led by Pitt, 'that great man': a complete contrast in his 'caution and moderation' to Robespierre. The picture is of a sound and healthy society, if at times a little absurd; but although Orczy may poke fun at the English 'John Bulls' who looked upon all foreigners with a 'withering contempt', the attitudes she herself expresses do not fall far short of theirs.

When his novels deal with a confrontation between England and a foreign power, Rafael Sabatini shows an equally clear bias towards England and the values the country is supposed to represent. His picture of the Spaniards in *The Hounds of God* (1928), for example, portrays them as having Fascist attitudes, in contrast with the essential decency of English attitudes. It is a book which presents the picture of English characteristics without the complexities of *The White Company*, while foregrounding English superiority over less favoured nations – in this case, Spain – and so it provides good examples of the kinds of qualities which the romance writers attributed to the English.

The very setting of *The Hounds of God* – Elizabethan England – calls upon the national pride of Sabatini's readers by invoking a golden age. Alun Howkins[23] has detected a shift from the Victorian fascination with 'medieval' England, with all its chivalric and paternalistic overtones, towards a celebration of 'Tudor England' as the period which epitomized English greatness. The change, beginning in the 1880s, received impetus from the popularity of J. A. Froude's historical essays, such as those printed in *Short Studies in Great*

Subjects in 1898.[24] 'Tudor England' as presented in history and literature from the end of the nineteenth century was not precisely the period during which the Tudor dynasty ruled: Howkins suggests that it was a 'construction' which covered the period between the later years of Elizabeth to the 1680s. He comments:

> The Tudor construction was an extraordinarily powerful one. Unlike the medievalist construction it encouraged expansion and worldliness. Its heroes were adventurers rather than knights . . .. Above all it was English.[25]

The power of the 'Tudor' myth can be seen in the way it infiltrated so many areas of social life, from the rediscovery of sixteenth- and seventeenth-century music[26] to the 'mock-Tudor' homes of the period from 1900 to the inter-war years when semi-detached houses with a panel of half-timbering were the staple of almost every suburb.

For Sabatini the construction proved a useful one for setting the natural wholesomeness and pragmatism of the English against the degeneracy and intolerance of the foreigner. *The Hounds of God* was set in the 1580s, the dawn of the golden age, when little England could be portrayed as heroic in facing the bullying might of Spain. In addition, Philip II seems not only to have started the war which led to the Armada's sailing, but actually to have forced it upon the 'far-sighted' English through his unsportsmanlike behaviour towards English Protestants marooned in Spain. The situation at the beginning of the book, which explains the causes of the war, thus sets up a sense of Spanish duplicity from the start.

There is a further dimension. The Spanish viewpoint is distorted by religion, the perverse logic of the church – just as that of Orczy's French was by politics. (In contrast, the attitudes of the English heroine are presented as based on reason and common sense.) The Spanish feel justified in acting in bad faith towards heretics. Thus the innocent English, sending aid to famine-stricken Galicia under safe-conduct, find that their sailors are arrested to 'languish' in the prisons of the Inquisition. This is not simply described with anti-religious (or anti-church) feeling of the kind demonstrated by Conan Doyle (though Sabatini also manifests this strongly in some of his books, such as *The Strolling Saint* (1913)); Spanish religious ideas are intermingled with some very interesting racist notions – an extreme version of a concept of heredity popular at the time when *The Hounds of God* was written, the late 1920s.

The story is about a clash of culture which enables Sabatini to demonstrate the sporting, outdoor virtues of the English nature as opposed to the suspect 'foreign' qualities of artistic proficiency and book-learning. Lady Margaret Trevannion, an English woman who is a natural athlete, loves dogs and horses, and prefers the open moorlands to the stuffy library where her scholar father spends his days, is courted by Gervase, an honest if somewhat imperceptive lad, but a brave and intelligent soldier. She, however, prefers the refugee from the Spanish Armada, Don Pedro, whom the Trevannions harbour for a time. He is courtly and artistic, skilled with the lute, and a natural linguist and poet.

These qualities are shown to be meretricious when Don Pedro has succeeded in sending word home and a ship arrives to take him back to Spain. He takes advantage of Margaret's friendship for him, and the unsuspecting freedom of her association with him, to have her abducted.

He intends to take her to his home and there marry her; but Frey Luis, the 'spiritual guide' of his ship, is concerned that his charge will damage his soul by marrying a heretic. Margaret, who believes a churchman must by definition be a good man and therefore her ally in condemning the crime against her, unsuspectingly increases his alarm; since she thinks him a friend and enjoys intellectual argument she discusses religion with him and, to his horror, puts forward such telling arguments on behalf of Protestantism that he feels his own faith threatened.

At the same time he feels an insidious attraction in Margaret's fresh beauty, so different from the more sensual good looks of his countrywomen. He begins to look upon her as a demon sent to tempt him. As a result he denounces her to the Inquisition as soon as the ship arrives in Spain.

The picture is not so very different from that presented by Doyle and Orczy. Gervase shows the same qualities of *naïveté*, bravery and honesty as can be seen in Sir Nigel and in Orczy's Lord Tony; and Margaret's qualities, though unusual in some ways for a heroine, are cut to the same 'English' pattern. The naturalness and freshness of her good looks, her love of the open air, her bravery, and, above all, the essential innocence that underlies her open, uncoquettish manner are foregrounded. They are qualities which associate her with Maude Loring in Conan Doyle's *The White Company* – another very English heroine.

Don Pedro, by contrast, is accomplished but shallow; and as for Frey Luis, he represents much of what Sabatini suggests is wrong with the Spanish temperament, compared with the English. The repression of natural feeling which leads him both to feel Margaret's attractions and to react against the feeling with horror, the spiritual arrogance which leads him to blame her for his state of mind, when she is all but unconscious of her looks and their effect, and the twisted mind which can see in Margaret a dangerous enemy bent on his destruction rather than the innocent victim of an outrage, who deserves his protection: all of these traits are mirrored in the attitudes of King Philip himself and his confessor, and can be seen as characteristically Spanish.

Typical, too, is the blind faith which cannot admit any attack. Frey Luis believes so firmly in his religion that he cannot admit the justice of an argument even when he feels it; he would rather believe himself tempted by the devil. His lack of rationality is linked with a self-perpetuating ignorance and superstition, for all his learning.

These attitudes are linked with an extreme racism which is all the more striking in the inter-war years when the notion of 'Eugenics' was popular. The very concept of 'English' qualities is connected with it. Here, however, it is an extreme version which is fore-grounded. Frey Luis talks to Pedro of the Jews, 'those armies of the powers of darkness', and the Moors, 'those other legionaries of Hell' (p.132). These racial groups have been exiled from Spain, but their taint remains in the impure heredity of many Spanish houses. All the more necessary, then, that those who are 'clean of blood' like Don Pedro should not mingle it with that of heretics.

These are attitudes which were not unknown in England by the 1920s. Racialist theories (and in particular the idea of a 'master race') had been expressed in the late nineteenth century by Houston Stewart Chamberlain, whose work provided a foundation for many of Hitler's ideas. There had already been evidence of anti-immigrant feeling (specifically, anti-Jewish) not only in Germany but in England, too, fanned by rising unemployment, already becoming a problem in the 1920s. In presenting such ideas as the creation of a distorted mind, the product of an unhealthy culture, Sabatini was by implication sounding a warning. Moderate praise of 'English' qualities was one thing; extreme forms of such racial feelings were themselves anti-English. Here, they are a symptom of Spanish bigotry.

Bigotry is shown as leading to self-deception and casuistry; Frey Luis twists every argument made by Margaret in front of the Inquisition, and only the fact that the Chief Inquisitor is an intelligent man saves Margaret for long enough to allow Gervase to locate and rescue her. His Herculean efforts on her behalf, culminating in the amazing ride which brings him to her prison in time to save her, convince Margaret that her English hero is preferable to her Spanish lover, however superficially accomplished. Don Pedro has notably failed to save her from the Inquisition; in fact, he has to do penance himself. By the time Gervase appears, Margaret is already thoroughly disenchanted with the Spaniards; and the reader has learned with her. English qualities may seem less glittering than Spanish accomplishments, but they are more worthy.

The Hounds of God therefore gives an image of Englishness which is very similar to that given by Conan Doyle and Orczy. Honesty, openness and shrewd commonsense are qualities with which all these writers endow the English; in this book emphasized by the grim picture of opposed qualities attributed to the Spanish.

And, though the English queen who represents the British government at this period may be more complex, volatile in mood and self-indulgent, she shares the shrewdness and glories in the openness, bravery and determination of her subjects; thus she has a particular value for Gervase himself, and for Francis Drake, who is presented as a man much like Gervase in his attitudes – not always scrupulous in his methods, but fundamentally sound in his aims. Moreover, she and her advisers are presented as 'far-sighted'; they do not wish to go to war, knowing what damage this might inflict on the people, and only do so because of Spain's insupportable provocation.

The dominant attitude evoked is one of unconditional admiration for England. It is presented as a nation of strongly individualistic men and women, ruled by a government which acts cautiously and in the best interests of the people. Essentially, it is the same picture as Orczy had already given. From the 1890s to the 1930s these writers, in many ways disparate in attitudes, had combined to give an image of Englishness which showed a society of free individuals in which rulers and ruled were bound together by mutual respect. Since each author chose a different period setting, the effect was to suggest that a cross-section of English society taken at any time from the Middle Ages onwards was bound to show this society in a process of evolution. The close relationship between this picture of society and that of a state developing towards modernity, discussed in Chapter 4, is obvious; and it is this, rather than the attitudes towards war, which seems to be the most important underlying significance.

In books such as these, then, a set of qualities which are not, perhaps, particularly glamorous, is attributed to the English, and the story itself shows them to be particularly effective. The method seems crude, but, as long as the books simply confirmed what the English already thought of themselves, it served its purpose. The end of the nineteenth century, however, saw the development of another aspect of Englishness, one with a greater emotional charge. This was the evocation of an intense nostalgia for an imaginary rural England which, though a purely fictional construct, must have appealed to two or three generations of English men and women as a sadly lost reality.

This is the sense of nostalgia for a 'deep England' to which Patrick Wright has referred: a feeling usually described with 'sub-lyricism' in 'a language of vague and evocative gesture'.[27] 'Deep England' is not only an image of England built up from signifiers such as white cliffs, trout streams, cricket, morning mists rising over rivers; it is usually, as Alun Howkins has remarked, specifically rural and drawn from the south of England.[28] Howkins's explanation is that the image was constructed between 1870 and 1900, at a time when the financial operations of the City of London were becoming more important in the British economy and the manufacturing industries of the north less so. London was achieving the centrality of importance which had hitherto been associated with the north, but this was at a time when its slums, its vice and its criminality were giving increasing cause for concern. In consequence, it was the countryside which surrounded London which became the 'essence of England':[29] 'Purity, decency, goodness, honesty, even "reality" itself are closely identified with the rural south'.[30]

This valuing of the south country and its links with a more innocent and cohesive past can be seen in much of the literature of the 1880s and 1890s and the early years of the twentieth century: for example, in the poetry of Rupert Brooke before the First World War, in the Georgian anthologies, and, especially, in the prose and poetry of Edward Thomas. According to Peter Brooker and Peter Widdowson: 'At least three over-lapping generations of poets can be identified as writing in a distinctly English tradition and as offering an image of Englishness to a wide middle-to-lower-class reading public in the years before the First World War.'[31]

In considering the function of one such image, that constructed in E. M. Forster's *Howard's End*, Brooker and Widdowson argue that it is used to 'compose a literary myth which can, in the pages of fiction, neutralise and drive back the encroaching reality of "London" or "suburbia"'.[32] 'Englishness' can be used as a counter-balance to a world without roots, where in one sense everything is in a continual state of flux, but in another everything becomes the same, smoothed over by modernity. For Howkins, however, 'Englishness' is a political concept; the rural population of England was seen to have a particular character: a 'group' character, according to George Sturt, the life of which was based on 'tradition'.[33] Although Sturt and others who valued 'tradition' as a cohesive force in rural society, such as Vaughan Williams and Cecil Sharp, might be critical of the contemporary political structure, the image tended to reinforce it: 'they gave credence to its existing political and social structure'.[34]

It is certainly possible to see in the images of England provided by historical romances written between 1890 and the Second World War something of both these functions. Readers attracted to the books because of their nostalgic picture of a traditional England received the political message as well. In one way, historical romance seems particularly suited to provide such a picture; the past setting is after all the site of the nostalgia, and the myth of a traditional rural society can simply displace any reclamation of a 'real' past in the text.

At the same time there is a contradiction here. In their accounts of the nostalgia which arises from too anxious a sense of modernity, Wright and Howkins show it to be sited in the present, not the past: the emotion is based on a sense of a life amongst the ruins, and on the preservation of remnants of a traditional past surviving into the contemporary world and seen as fragile and threatened. How can the feeling of nostalgia be triggered when the past is portrayed as the present, as it is in historical romances?

This contradiction is resolved in many of the texts by distancing devices which preserve the sense that the action, though experienced by the reader as happening in the present, none the less takes place in a past sufficiently distant to evoke nostalgia; these devices also provide a means by which the excluded groups mentioned earlier (see p.67) can identify with the picture of deep England. One such device is the use of a narrator who finds that the action of the story triggers his own nostalgia for a purer yet more colourful world. The narrator of Stanley Weyman's *Under the Red Robe* (1894), riding on a mission for Cardinal Richelieu which will help him to continue enjoying 'power, pleasure, life, everything worth winning' (p.77) in Paris, is led by the freshness of the Béarnese countryside with its 'silence', 'clear brooks' and 'glades still green' to remember his innocent Breton childhood and to feel that his present work as the Cardinal's spy is inglorious: 'not a gentleman's work' (p.31).

This device is one used frequently by A. E. W. Mason. Lawrence Clavering, for example, in the book of that name,[35] looks back upon England with a sense of acute loss. At the beginning of the book it is clear that he had been educated in Paris, and only an accident brings him to England. His time there is uncomfortable; yet when he finally settles in Avignon, married to the woman he loves and with everything, it would seem, to make him happy, the memory of Blackladies, his Cumbrian home, is so potent that he sees visions of it in the Rhône, and is 'touched for the moment to a foolish melancholy' (p.7).

Foolish it may be, but it is clear that he feels a sense of exile in 'a country of tourelles'. He longs for 'the brown hills' of Cumberland, even though they were the setting for his most disastrous adventures and, moreover, he has carried off to Avignon what he most valued there – his wife, Dorothy.

Mason's method here is not unlike that of Orczy, Sabatini and Conan Doyle in their recommendation of English qualities. There seems to be nothing intrinsically lovable about brown hills, yet through Clavering's expressions of loss the reader is given the impression that there is something special about them, perhaps akin to the qualities attributed to English men and women. They may not be eyecatching, but there is a sense of wholesomeness about the phrase, and, perhaps, of understated strength, which makes the feminine-sounding 'tourelles' seem artificial and flimsy.

The narrator's nostalgia in both these books is one of the interpellative devices which draw the reader into the constructed identity of the hero and endow him or her temporarily with memories of Béarn or Cumbria. These memories provide the reader with a sense of having a rightful title to the aristocratic and masculine tradition of 'Englishness'; Patrick Wright argues plausibly that 'To be a subject of Deep England is above all to have *been there*',[36] but this experience can be simulated for the reader as can any other.

Another device is that of setting a distance momentarily between the reader and the action of the story, so that the reader becomes aware of the action as having taken place a long time ago. Weyman, for instance, uses this at the end of *The Castle Inn* (1898): concluding a story full of contested inheritances, abduction and near-rape, whirlwind pursuits and hair's-breadth escapes, the author reminds the reader that the Castle Inn still stands in Marlborough. The reader can walk along the very roads along which the hero and heroine wandered and fell in love. The note is that of a pastoral idyll rather than the conclusion of a story of suspense, and expresses the kind of pleasant sadness which comes from contemplating the passage of time. It also suggests that the story has been one episode in a continuing tradition: the Castle Inn, part of our own world, was part of the world of Sir George Soan and his lover all those years ago. The place provides a link between the hero and the 1890s; all the reader of that period had to do to earn a title to the aristocratic tradition of which Sir George was a part was to visit Marlborough.

Jeffrey Farnol uses a similar device to draw the reader into a past which from the very beginning is seen from a nostalgic distance. *The Broad Highway* (1910) begins with a prologue in which the author, tramping English lanes, meets a tinker with decided views on what should go into a romance. The ingredients he mentions – 'dooks or earls, or barro-nites', 'a little blood', and 'some love' – are important features of the genre and are incorporated into the story, but the atmosphere is set by the author, preferring to write of 'country things and ways and people' (p.2).

The context of this 'Ante-Scriptum', the author's walk through the countryside, with its echoes of W. H. Hudson, evokes rural England as a focus for nostalgic contemplation. The initial image is one in which the author tramps through contemporary English lanes, but once it becomes apparent that the tinker to whom he has been talking is one of the characters from his eighteenth-century story the 'author' is drawn into the past too, together with his landscape; past and present are fused, and the reader's modern urbanized world becomes the rural world of the eighteenth century, while at the same time the artificiality of the device sets the reader at a distance from the story and enables story and setting to be seen through a nostalgic haze.

Farnol uses the past as a nostalgic frame for a world which never existed in fact: an impossible 'old England' untouched by the industrial revolution. He is not concerned to produce an accurate picture of pre-industrialized Britain; his England is simply what the modern world is not, a gentle, countrified background for private adventure.

He includes almost no public conflict; his is an England at peace, though there are suggestions of a heroic recent past of a nature in keeping with 'English' qualities. Sir Richard Anstruther, the hero's guardian, for instance, is the 'type' of an English country gentleman who has fearlessly confronted death on 'the littered quarterdeck of reeking battleships' and 'the smoke and death of stricken fields', but who now passes his days happily among turnips and cabbages (p.13). His experience links him with the humble men who fought with him as common soldiers: Tom Price the carrier, for example, who fought in the Peninsular war, saving his officer's life and being set up afterwards in business by him. For the readers of 1910 who feared the prospect of war, the book therefore offered a peaceful world, but one in which fighting, safely in the past, has provided an achievement of which Englishmen could be proud, and which has to some extent united all social classes.

In general, however, it is the peaceful beauty of the countryside rather than the fighting, however noble, which is stressed. Farnol's picture is idyllic, like his description of the Oxford road in *The High Adventure* (1926): 'a white, dusty highway shaded, here and there, by stately trees' which went 'past crawling country wains . . . past plodding wayfarers . . . past shady wood and purling rill . . . past fragrant rickyards where busy fowls clucked and smock-frocked figures turned to stare' (p.279). The parklike suggestion of 'shady trees' frames a picture which could have been drawn by an eighteenth-century landscape artist, with a wealth of picturesque detail but anything that might suggest poverty, hard work or filth left out. The archaic, slightly poetic diction, which was not altogether unusual in this period – Sabatini uses it too, for instance, especially in dialogue[37] – but which was a particular hallmark of Farnol's style, adds to the impression, which seems designed to lend the past a warm, sentimental glow.

A country village in Farnol's England is portrayed as manageably small: 'some half-dozen cottages with roofs of thatch, or red tile, backed by trees gnarled and ancient'. Here, 'characters' like the

Ancient in *The Broad Highway* – childlike, opinionated, yet lovable, a kind of idealized grandfather – or Black George – the gigantic blacksmith who can fell a man with a blow and yet, when he is not tormented by jealousy, is a gentle man and a loyal friend – live out their lives. They may not be significant figures on the national stage, yet in the village setting they are men of importance, as is every individual who lives there, since the village is shown as a tiny world in itself, though linked with a hundred others as complete and self-enclosed. The past, too – a purely local one – lives on here in the memory of the old people, to become legend in due course, like the story of the suicide who built Peter Vibart's cottage in *The Broad Highway*.

Within the limits of the village society, Farnol portrays a world which may contain individual, private conflicts, but no social conflict. The villagers respect the gentry, but do not envy them. Black George, for example, is honestly glad to hear that Peter is a gentleman of fortune, although he feels that this distances Peter from him, as though a gentleman were another order of being; he wants to wash his hands before shaking Peter's, even though he had shaken them often enough before without any such fuss. Peter, on the other hand shows that he values George's friendship and the dirt which is the fruit of his honest toil by insisting on shaking George's hand just as it is. An image of mutual respect and loyalty has been built up which contrasts with that of the fashionable yet treacherous world of Peter's cousin, Maurice Vibart. The book thus resembles other texts which construct an image of 'Englishness' implying a respect for every individual that transcends class, such as Conan Doyle's *The White Company*.

Certainly, in turning his back on Sir Richard's world at the beginning of the book, to live in Sissinghurst, Peter does not leave Sir Richard's 'English' values behind him: his generosity, loyalty, bravery and love of the land. Such qualities belong to the true gentlemanly code, which in Farnol's work shows an affinity with Conan Doyle's chivalry and the feminine, Huguenot qualities promoted by Weyman. By the time of *The Broad Highway*, the chivalric paraphernalia beloved of the Victorians might no longer be in fashion, but its values can be seen as assumptions, not only in the work of Farnol, but also in that of later writers who developed the 'Georgian myth', like Warwick Deeping. In Farnol's books this myth can be seen to have a similar function to chivalry in Conan Doyle's, since 'gentlemanliness' amongst the landlords means a contented peasantry, and none of those social discontents which at the time could be seen to disrupt the social fabric in the form of the contemporary series of strikes.

In showing a paternalistic, aristocratic and contented society Farnol was showing as already achieved the state to which the societies of other romancers, such as Weyman, were aspiring. There is a hint in Conan Doyle's work that this kind of integrated society is a feature of English society in particular: French society is shown as much more class-ridden and full of conflict than England, and the code of chivalry, though international, seems most recognized in England. If there is any class conflict in Conan Doyle's England it is presented as the fault of a basically foreign aristocracy which is becoming naturalized as the commons grow freer.

This tendency to see free and contented lower classes as particularly English is part of the strongly nationalistic sentiment which Conan Doyle, and after him Orczy, Sabatini and Farnol, create. 'Englishness', in all these authors, is above all a collection of qualities which, together, prove the virtues of the English form of government.

If England could be shown to have been a society of free commoners, protected by traditional rights and respected by their natural governors – the aristocracy in previous centuries and the middle classes, originally agents of the governors, in the nineteenth and twentieth – the effect is to suggest that little change is needed.

*

If it is natural to find a concept of Englishness which is strongly linked with masculinity in the work of Farnol, Sabatini, Weyman, Mason and Conan Doyle, such a concept seems to have less place in the work of a female writer producing books for a feminine market like Georgette Heyer. Her early books, however, are male-centred like those of the earlier romancers and do draw upon the familiar 'English' characteristics. There are, however, differences between the function of 'Englishness' in her work and in earlier historical romances; it has less connection with the creation of nationalist feeling and more with the development of an ideal of masculinity. In her later books any vestigial traces of the concept were therefore subsumed by the figure of the romantic hero.

To illustrate this it is helpful to compare one aspect of 'Englishness' as it is found in her work with the way it is used in earlier romances. This is that 'tendency' of Anglo-Saxons to believe that if anyone behaved badly they must be some 'form of foreigner', already mentioned in connection with the work of Conan Doyle (see p.69). In the books by Conan Doyle and Orczy in which this feeling is most clearly expressed it is the French above all who are compared unfavourably with the English. Conan Doyle's French knights are, with some honourable exceptions like du Guesclin, boastful and snobbish, and Orczy shows even royalist Frenchmen as touchily protective of a false sense of honour, like the little Vicomte in *The Scarlet Pimpernel*, or apt to forget honour in pursuit of love, like Margeurite Blakeney's brother Armand in *The Triumph of the Scarlet Pimpernel*.

Georgette Heyer draws upon a different set of associations: those connected with French style. From the time of the Restoration, when exiled Royalists came back full of the French tastes and fashions which Etherege and Congreve were to mock, the English *beau monde* (the very name is significant) looked to the French as natural leaders of fashion. The Frenchified Englishman in literature had more polish than, say, an English country gentleman, but the polish could cover a good deal of absurdity and ill-nature as well, as is the case with Etherege's Sir Fopling Flutter or Vanbrugh's Lord Foppington. 'France' is here connected with an excessive interest in fashion which leads the fop to abrogate his 'natural' masculinity. Narcissistic and valuing appearance rather than power, the Frenchified fop has qualities akin to the 'split' self which John Berger has seen as a characteristic of socially constructed femininity: 'A woman . . . is almost continually accompanied by her own image of herself.'[38]

This element of 'femininity' in the presentation of upper-class Frenchmen by the English outlasted the Restoration. In the 1940s the foppishness of the French court made a ridiculous contrast with the shabby but brave English army in Olivier's film of *Henry V*. In the same tradition, Heyer's over-fashionable fops are as absurd as those in any Restoration comedy. If some of them are redeemed to become heroic, it is because – and in this Heyer follows Baroness Orczy with her foppish Sir Percy Blakeney – their foppishness is assumed as a cover for a genuinely 'English' manliness. Heyer, however, goes further: the foppishness is not merely a cover, it expresses a part of their nature which in fact has its own heroic aspect.

This blend of 'English' masculinity with 'French' style can be seen in Heyer's first novel, *The Black Moth* (1921). The story is centred around a hero who, having been exiled from English society after a gaming scandal, has assumed the identity of 'Sir Anthony Ferndale', a gentleman who spends much of his life in France. 'Sir Anthony' shocks his very British lawyer with his French mannerisms and unmasculine dress: a 'full-skirted coat of palest lilac laced with silver', 'shoes with high red heels' and 'a huge emerald' flashing on his finger (p.5). In front of the lawyer he flounces and lards his words with French expressions.

This foppish persona is a cover for his real identity as Jack Carstares, heir to the Earl of Wyncham, which is that of an honourable Englishman. His masculine strength and vigour still appear amidst his mannerisms, for instance in the way he opens the door before mincing in to tease his lawyer. His exile springs from the sense of honour which led to him taking the blame for his brother Richard's cheating at cards, so that Richard can marry the woman they both love. He will never admit his innocence in case he breaks up Richard's home, and he will never even admit to the hurt he feels in being exiled from society, since he has a manly dislike of showing his feelings. He feels such a display would be a weakness which could lead him into dishonour; when the heroine confesses her love for him, he will not respond even though the strength of the feeling he is repressing makes him turn pale and feel faint. He is a powerful fighter and his sense of chivalry sends him into battle more than once to rescue the heroine.

These are the traits of a 'genuine' Englishman, admirable as long as his 'feminine' Frenchified foppishness is seen as a mask which can easily be discarded – as Sir Percy Blakeney's foppishness had been. At the same time, there is a sense in which foppishness is a genuine trait of Jack's. Throughout the book he worries about his clothes and appearance, even when he is badly wounded, and the vanity which leads him to tend his hands and keep them white and well-trimmed leads also to the destruction of another of his personae, that of a highwayman. This fits a 'feminine' side of his personality which otherwise only finds expression in his 'rather wistful' eyes (p.5). It is this side of him which draws the heroine to him: it gives him a sympathy with her concerns which makes him an interesting and charming companion, and lies behind the chivalry which sends him to her rescue.

Masculine Englishness and feminine 'Frenchness' are thus presented as coming together to form a well-balanced personality: a conjunction to be found in other books by Heyer, such as *Powder and Patch* (1923). In this novel the very English hero is sent to Paris to learn foppery before he is a fit mate for the heroine.

From the 1890s to the 1930s the writers of historical romance, in many ways disparate in attitude, showed a remarkable similarity in their protrayal of 'English' qualities. The image of England as the home of chivalry, tolerance and imperial duty seems so suited to the context of the end of the nineteenth century, when the first seeds of economic decline, masked as it was by imperial success, were beginning to shoot, that it is surprising to find it still flourishing in books of the 1920s. It is also a masculine image; yet features of it are to be found in the work of Georgette Heyer, a woman author writing for a female audience. That one concept should be found in work of different periods, and used in later novels for a very different purpose in creating a kind of romantic hero who is particularly appealing to women, suggests its potency and adaptability. 'Englishness' may change its form to suit changing circumstances, but over the years it has retained its main features, and is still strong in its power to appeal to the public, as current debates about the role of Britain in Europe, and as a multi-cultural state, attest.

Chapter 6

Class, the gospel of work and 'hazard'

In Chapter 4 it was argued that at a time when the liberal bourgeois state was increasing in power, historical romances were presenting images of past governments which suggested that such a state was the culmination of a natural and healthy development. These images had national and social dimensions: the 'healthy develop-ment' was presented as a particularly English phenomenon, and the natural leadership of such a state was vested in a beneficent upper class.

The beneficence was part of the larger constellation of qualities which went to make up the Victorian ideal of a gentleman. This was based on the Victorian concept of chivalry which, as Marc Girouard argued, was first fully articulated by Kenelm Digby in *The Broad-stone of Honour* (1832).[1] It was a concept which had a strong moral dimension: honour, particularly in the sense of trustworthiness, protectiveness towards the weak and poor, and the ability to put the needs of others before one's own were important aspects of it. A gentleman needed fighting skills to protect the weak – chivalry was a strongly masculine concept – but aggression without due cause was wrong; self-control was an important aspect too.

It was his chivalrous qualities, rather than his Norman blood, which fitted Sir Nigel in Conan Doyle's *The White Company* for leadership in a land of freeborn Englishmen like Samkin Aylward or Hordle John. Sir Nigel respects the qualities of these two men and they are his friends; but there is a qualitative difference between them. In the historical romances of the 1890s and 1900s, gentle and simple are shown as linked by strong bonds of affection, loyalty and responsibility, but divided by boundaries which either tried to cross not only at their peril but to the danger of the whole of society.

The relationship between ruled and rulers is an important theme of the 'adventure' romances, from Conan Doyle, writing in the 1890s, to Sabatini and Orczy, who were still writing in the 1930s (Sabatini published books in the 1950s). 'Female- orientated' romance of the kind written by Heyer and her followers was more concerned with the world of a glamorized aristocracy whose lifestyle provided an opportunity for escape, but I would argue that even their world was seen as underpinned by similar values. In the 1970s and 1980s, however, some writers began to present a less favourable picture of the aristocracy: one which suggested they were decadent and not really fitted for their wealth and status. To be deserved, wealth should be earned: one finds in the work of writers such as Mira Stables or Mary Ann Gibb a positive valuation of such qualities as hard work and trustworthiness in business, together with a favourable image of business acumen.

This model of society, which is unequal but not unfair since the rewards of wealth and status go to the deserving, may well have been based on attitudes which were becoming more widely diffused in the years immediately before the coming to power of the radical Right under Mrs Thatcher, and which grew in strength during the 1980s. I would argue, however, that it is not a model which can easily co-exist with other aspects of historical romance, and its contradictions are exposed in the texts through a number of features, in particular the use of chance – especially in the form of gambling – rather than desert to resolve situations which arise from the unfairness of society.

The image of society presented by the texts thus reveals both continuity and transformation. How these various images are constructed, and how they relate to each other, I hope to show in an account of three novels, one from the 1900s and two from the 1970s and 1980s.

*

In all the romances of the 1890s and 1900s the upper classes may be strongly criticized, and the lower classes shown as in some senses better, but the boundaries between the classes remain rigid and the hierarchy is never seriously questioned; in fact, any criticism seems rather to confirm it, as when Conan Doyle shows the king behaving rudely to a serf, who is then condemned for his resentment.

A. E. W. Mason, in particular, gives the impression that the lower classes actually belong to a different species from that of the gentry, and one that is markedly inferior. His books rarely contain any presentation of productive labour, and the working class appears in a limited range of roles, almost all connected with service.

The Courtship of Morrice Buckler (1901) is the book which comes closest to portraying a working-class community, and here the attitude is one of contempt and disgust. The hero, Morrice Buckler, kills the Count of Lukstein in a duel in revenge for the death of his friend, destroyed by the Count. Buckler's own behaviour, in attempting first to save his friend, and then putting his own life in danger to avenge him, is honourable and gentlemanly to a high degree. When, later, he meets and falls in love with the widowed Countess, it is this scrupulous sense of honour which stops him from shaming her by telling her that her husband had been unfaithful, and, in shielding her from the knowledge, he puts himself in danger; for despite the Count's unsavoury character, and the fact that she never loved him, her own sense of upper-class honour leads the Countess to mourn him and plan vengeance in her turn. She lures Buckler to her castle, and has him kidnapped and placed in the custody of a small group of woodcutters who live on the mountainside close to Lukstein. There she intends to keep him prisoner until she feels that reparation has been made for her husband's death.

These woodcutters are an extreme example of 'brutal' working-class characters as portrayed in the romances. The implication of the portrayal is that their aspirations towards autonomy need not be taken seriously: indeed, it is questionable whether they have any. They are bound to the Countess by ties of service, and so fulfil a kind of feudal role. They may actually be her servants; certainly their obedience to her is absolute. They hold Buckler prisoner at her orders, apparently without question; and her servant Grober works alongside them as of right. In winter they live in a nearby village. There are four or five houses and an inn, where the woodcutters frequently get drunk. Even in the village the Countess's will rules, for if the woodcutters get too drunk to stand guard, 'there were ever some cottagers from the neighbouring cottages ready to fill their place' (p.334).

The impression given is of a medieval vassalage, and there is no suggestion that this system might be outdated in the second half of the seventeenth century when the story takes place, or unfair. It is made to seem part of the natural order. The Countess is a superior person; the peasants are inferior by nature – coarser, with almost animal habits. Their 'greasy steaming gruel' and 'dry coarse bread' and 'spirit of a very bitter flavour' are things Buckler, the gentleman, has to 'constrain' himself to eat (p.327).

The gruel forms the 'chief food' of the woodcutters, but there is no suggestion that *they* are badly treated in having to live on such awful food while the Countess banquets in the castle. If anything, they are blamed for their diet, and for forcing it upon Buckler, as though it were their own choice arising from degraded tastes. Their occupations – felling trees in summer and ropemaking in winter – are 'tedious and mechanic labour' for Buckler (p.328), a hardship of a terrible nature from which he must escape; but again it is not suggested that there is anything wrong with a system which enforces a lifetime of such labour upon his fellow human beings.

Instead, the reader gains the impression that the peasants are well-suited to their work. Their conversation consists of 'rough jests and songs' (p.335), but they have nothing to say to Buckler; in any case, they are often too drunk to talk to him. To Buckler, the idea that he might become like these peasants is the most horrifying aspect of his imprisonment: that he might sink into 'a dull apathy . . . until I became one with these coarse peasants in spirit and mind . . . ignorant boors' (p.330).

Such pictures of lower-class characters are as common in later romance as at the turn of the century. Jeffrey Farnol is perhaps unusual in allowing individuality of a kind to his working-class men and women. Characters such as 'the Ancient' and 'Black George', who inhabit the village of Sissinghurst in *The Broad Highway* (1910), are full of quirks of character which the hero recognizes and enjoys, while valuing the friendship of men who are essentially good and trustworthy. On the other hand, these characters have a childlike quality about them which makes it difficult to take them seriously.

Farnol himself held fairly radical social attitudes and in this, his first novel, he makes his hero express a preference for honest work ('digging') over the life of an idle gentleman. He actually becomes a blacksmith for a time, but it is noticeable that once he inherits his uncle's money he leaves his job and the village as soon as he can.

In the same way, a more recent romantic writer, Eva Macdonald, declares her sympathy with lower-class concerns, but agrees with other authors in valuing lower-class characters for their loyalty and usefulness to the gentry. In *Cromwell's Spy* (1976) she comments that it is not in the interests of the peasantry to support the king's party; however, she later writes approvingly of a servant who sacrifices herself to save her master's silver plate from the hands of an unscrupulous Parliamentarian: an approval which is at variance with her earlier comment.

Even the expression of interest in lower-class concerns is rare in contemporary romance. For the most part the notion that lower and upper classes are members of different species, fixed naturally and forever in their respective social positions, is so much taken for granted that the texts never present it for examination. It is an attitude which lies behind such an episode as the meeting of the hero and heroine in Clare Darcy's *Letty* (1980). The hero comes across Letty in the street, dressed like a servant, but despite appearances he recognizes her at once as an aristocrat because of the fineness of her features.

The continuance of this picture of a fixed social hierarchy with a gulf between the classes and based on a natural distinction is one of the most enduring features of historical romance – sufficiently so to give the impression that one of the attractions of the past setting lies in this. It is a part of that traditional world whose passing is, in Patrick Wright's words, 'experienced in terms of loss'.[2] The developing class structure of twentieth-century England, with its less clearcut boundaries,[3] may have led to the idea, supported by 'a chorus of authoritative voices'[4] in the 1950s and resurrected in the 1990s by John Major, that essentially England was becoming a classless society; and though this may seem progressive, and a sounder base for a social democracy in which traditional class conflict has become outdated, it can at the same time be experienced as part of the dislocating character of modernity, particularly if it can be seen as linked to a breakdown of traditional values. Although this may appear ironic (since the evidence of such studies as Margaret Stacey's Banbury surveys suggests that 'the whole of the class set-up . . . went cheerfully on its way, just as elaborately stratified as ever'),[5] it helps to explain why a traditional class stratification may have been part of the pleasure of the nostalgic backward glance offered by the romances.

Consequently there is very little suggestion in the romances that it is possible to move from class to class. Latterly, however, in the 1970s and 1980s, a number of romances have begun to give approving portraits of upwardly mobile characters, especially when they can be seen to rise through their own efforts. These seem to appeal to more divided feelings. On the one hand the world of the past is still presented as a glamorous pre-industrial society where all the upper classes needed to do was to enjoy themselves in a sort of perpetual holiday; on the other, a certain resentment towards the welfare state as a haven for scroungers which left those whose efforts most supported it unable to enjoy the fruits of their labours – a resentment which came to a head in the election of 1979 – can be seen reflected in the emphasis these books place on the distribution of reward to the deserving.

In these books, parables for the new age, the desert which is rewarded is a combination of hard work and independence. Thus Eva Macdonald's poverty-stricken heroine in *House of Secrets* (1980) finds work in a tea-shop and eventually comes to own not only this but a superior establishment which is one of the foremost in the West End. Independence is one of her most obvious characteristics; she will not even let anyone carry her case for her, even when she has to struggle with it. Sheila Bishop's heroine in *The Phantom Garden* (1974) has become one of England's leading singers in the London of the eighteenth century; she, too, has risen from relative poverty and is not even aristocratic by birth – though she has been brought up from childhood in an upper-class house. And in Mary Ann Gibb's *A Most Romantic City* (1976), a banker whose fortune has come from putting his wife's money to use is portrayed with approval, especially when it is made clear that his speculation was carried out with a most scrupulous honesty.

The typical values of the aristocratic world of the romances are thus overlaid in these books by others, more suited to their times, of hard work, competitiveness and honesty: a trinity which is seen to succeed in a society which is essentially fair. Rewards go to those fittest to survive in the economic jungle, but the fittest are also the most virtuous and deserving. In many ways these attitudes are more akin to those of the mid-nineteenth century than to those of Conan Doyle or Weyman or their followers at the end of the century.

Such features, and their contradictions, can be seen in an analysis of two books by Mira Stables, an author particularly concerned to promote the virtues of hard work.

*

The later of these two novels, *Golden Barrier* (1981), is also the most explicit. Praise for the man who is upwardly mobile through his own efforts in one of the book's most notable features. Near the beginning of the story, which is set in England in the early nineteenth century, the heroine, a rich but rather plain heiress, refuses an offer of marriage from an impoverished aristocrat. She suspects him of loving her money more than herself, and the suspicion leads her to outline her attitudes fully and clearly.

Despite his fortune-hunting, the suitor, Lord Sandiland, is genuinely fond of the heroine, Kate Martenhays. He says that he hopes to support her as his wife, but, not having the means to do so, he proposes to do it on her money. Kate also expects her husband to support her, if only in modest comfort, but he must make, not marry, the money to do it with. She explains that her husband will not despise 'honest toil' but will 'work and study' for prosperity (p.22).

No doubt is cast on the excellence of such values. Both Kate and Sandiland agree that such a husband would be an ideal, a 'paragon'. Even though Sandiland clearly intends to stay as far away from 'honest toil' as he can, he none the less acknowledges its value. However, there is no question – as there might have been in a Jeffrey Farnol romance – of equating work with manual labour. During the scene in which Sandiland proposes, Kate clarifies the meaning of 'toil' in this context: her husband will be 'hardworking' because he will 'set the money to work to make more' – which means, presumably, that she sees him as a banker like her father – and he will also set his children to work.

This attitude, reminiscent of Samuel Smiles's praise for self-help, belongs to a Regency heroine who has more in common with the nascent manufacturing world and with finance than with the life of a 'frivolous society damsel', a life of which, as she tells her father later in the novel, she has become heartily tired. The reader is likely to sympathize, even if she originally picked up the book with the expectation of reading a society romance, since the very first scene of the book has already shown a fashionable family in a very poor light.

The book opens with a visit by Kate, while she was still a child, to her aristocratic and fashionable neighbours in the country, the Dorseys. The children of the house, bored with her company, had left her in the stables while they went off riding. Kate, who had scarcely even seen a horse before, was terrified, and, almost distraught, had to be rescued by the children's cousin, Dermot Winfield.

The young aristocrats behaved brutally, not because they were malicious, but because they were frivolous and sensation-seeking.

The girl loved riding, and the ride would take her to the village where she could flirt with one of the villager's sons. Her brother wanted to meet his friends for sport. The heartlessness and falsity of a system of values which could place such pleasures before their duty to their guest are made quite clear; the author allows the reader a glimpse of the motives of brother and sister, but the viewpoint is mainly that of the heroine so that the reader must perforce share her feelings of social uncertainty, embarrassment and, finally, outright fear.

The sense of the heroine's vulnerability does not last; in the scene with Sandiland it is clear that she has grown into a forceful young woman with a mind of her own. She now represents economic power, not Cinderella-like pathos. When she later returns to the countryside of her childhood, the reader learns that the young aristocrats have come to grief, their fortune is wasted, and the boy has died. Kindly cousin Dermot, the poor relation, has inherited their property, but without the money to maintain it – what money remaining in the family possession having been willed to Lady Dorsey.

In this context, the little prologue takes on a different aspect. The vulnerable little girl can be seen as representative of a new class, lacking power at first but, as she grows, becoming powerful enough to take the place of the old landed gentry. The old gentry, by contrast, has forfeited the right to power and privilege; the frivolity and selfishness of the young sister and brother are signs of effeteness rather than of inherent ill-nature.

Kate has links with both the old gentry and the new world of manufacturing and finance, but feels herself more akin to the latter. Her father is a rich banker, now living the life of a country gentleman but still anxious to put his capital to work. Kate sympathizes with his aspirations, an approval which is itself evidence of this novel's break with the traditions of the genre. In Georgette Heyer's *A Civil Contract* (1961), for instance, the heroine's rich father is a vulgarian trying to push his daughter into titled society, and a similar situation and characterization are to be found as late as 1974 in Barbara Cartland's *The Bored Bridegroom*. Such attitudes were perhaps more in keeping with pre-industrial upper-class ones than those portrayed in *Golden Barrier*, but the latter are more likely to appeal to a twentieth-century readership, even if historically incorrect. This is because the twentieth-century aristocracy was the result of the process of 'bourgeoisification' which according to Anthony

Giddens was the 'most striking characteristic' of the British upper class in the late nineteenth century,[6] a culmination of a process which had its roots in the seventeenth. The attitudes towards the *nouveau riche* portrayed by Heyer and Cartland probably show a better empathy with the Regency, but a twentieth-century readership could more easily recognize an upper class which comprised not only the landed gentry but other groups such as industrial and financial magnates and members of the 'top' professions. If Stables's historicism is suspect, therefore, her contemporary relevance is greater.

The approval of the world of finance suggested by Kate's description of her ideal husband is underlined later by a conversation she has with her father after declining Sandiland's proposal; she begs him to let her give up the life of a London socialite and live with him in the country, and help him in his transactions. In London society she feels marginalized and valueless because of her awareness of new economic developments: 'all that is going on in the world today'. She declares herself 'proud' of what her father has achieved: that is, to amass wealth.

On her mother's side, however, she comes from the old gentry. This family, by Martenhay's account, had been as shiftless and weak as their erstwhile neighbours. The grandparents had been poor. Facing bankruptcy, they had refused to consent to the marriage of their daughter with a socially inferior banker, though the bank could have 'bought them up ten times over'. Their son-in-law has little sympathy with their lack of greed; Martenhays seems to feel they should be condemned as snobs, and also – which is interesting – as impractical. The impression is given that it was their duty to rescue themselves from poverty in whatever way they could, especially since they were 'poverty poor'.

Wealth, then, is to be commended, if achieved by individual hard work; the old aristocracy, revealed as weak and shiftless, deserves its poverty. One exception to this is Dermot, the new owner of the Priory, the house which Kate had visited as a little girl. He too has mixed roots, connected through his mother with the Dorseys, but the child of a *mésalliance* and brought up very much as a poor relation. Despite his connections, therefore, his position at the Priory is that of Martenhays in his youth, that of a man with his own way to make in the world. Like Martenhays, too, he is far from feeling shame in hard work: to make his home farm pay he is 'always there where the work's heaviest and hardest' (p.42), as an admiring employee observes. He is thus linked to Kate by the way in which he belongs to two worlds, the old and the new, as well as by his kindness to her when she was a child.

His position changes when Kate, secretly helping to mend the worn tapestries at the Priory in order to practise her skills with the needle, finds some lost jewels, hidden in the tapestry. Possessions of the Dorsey family, they should have passed to Dermot through his mother.

Dermot is now tolerably rich, but once he realizes he owes his good fortune to Kate his pride rebels and a hostility grows up between them. It is only when Dermot is able to save Kate from the harassment of a group of wandering tinkers that this is resolved. He begins to think of her as a suitable wife, admiring the desire for useful work which set her to mending his tapestries – a feeling which ranges her with her father and himself as members of the new, utilitarian world – but her fortune remains a barrier between them. To marry her would be to make himself wealthy without his own efforts, and in any case he knows she has strong views about fortune-hunters.

He is clearly nothing of the kind. Martenhays, as he gets to know him, sees in him a worthy heir who will make the most of the banker's fortune if he has it under his control. Once he has his small fortune from the sale of the jewels, Dermot wants to make modern improvements on his land which will enable him to run it more profitably, but he is anxious to provide alternative work for any redundant labourers by building a knitting mill: a venture which will also bring new wealth to him and to Martenhays, who becomes his partner ("'No reason why you should not show a respectable profit'").

The rest of the book shows how the impasse of the 'golden barrier' is overcome when Dermot once again saves Kate, this time from a ruined reputation: the fortune-hunting Sandiland has abducted her in the hope of blackmailing her into marriage. He only precipitates the wedding between Kate and his rival. The new man, now tested and proved to be a worthy heir to capitalist enterprise, gains Kate, her wealth, and retains his ancient aristocratic home as well.

The Priory, like England herself, has become home again to the really useful rich, and the gold, far from being a barrier, is set free to bring prosperity to all who, in their turn, show themselves willing to deserve it by working for Dermot and Martenhays. The novel's title provides a central image, not just for the love story, but – perhaps more potently – for the economic theme: that gold, unused, is of as little use to the parched countryside as a river which has been dammed up, but, once the barrier is lowered, the streams of gold can bring fertility to everything around. Capital and the profit motive together bring this about: Dermot needs money to maintain his life-style; Martenhays wants a decent return on his capital and feels that by helping Dermot he is backing a winner. There is a strong suggestion that without *their* needs for wealth and grandeur, the more modest needs of the lower classes for comfort and nourishment would never be met. If there is inequality here, it is made necessary by the very nature of things.

For the financier and the manufacturer, working together, have become the new guardians of society, replacing the discredited aristocracy. Poverty – loosely defined – is the trap from which all the characters except Kate have to attempt, at one time or another, to escape. The only way to do so is to use capital if one has it or to sell labour to those who are willing to use it. Those who follow the new leaders are good and are rewarded, and all those who, in their different stations in life, reject their go-getting spirit of enterprise are left to suffer.

Whether the unenterprising are Viscounts (like Sandilands), earls' children (like the Dorseys) or lower-class, they remain, however, an irritating element in society. The economic body would be healthier without them. This is made clear by the portrayal of the tinkers who, by frightening Kate, first bring her and the adult Dermot together.

They are a poverty-stricken lot. Lower-class poverty is worse than the shiftless middle-class version represented by Kate's grandparents. These tinkers are a dreadful group. Two of them have been stealing, and it is made clear that they are all scroungers, putting on an act in order to con the unwary into giving them food and shelter which they are too lazy to work for. Kate herself falls into this trap, giving them shelter in her father's barn and bringing them food, but the discovery of the thief makes her realize how wrong she was; she is in fact embarrassed at being found helping such an unworthy group. Their attitude becomes threatening, and she becomes thoroughly frightened. In rescuing her, Dermot has to threaten them in his turn with the law, a language they understand and respect. Kate learns her lesson: human kindness is thrown away on the undeserving.

Perhaps it is because the message of this book is so clearly stated that the paradox of romantic episodes running counter to the theme of desert is here particularly noticeable. Despite all the praise of hard work, very little of it is actually described in the story. Country houses, old families, and the fashionable world of London society which Kate professes to despise provide the attractive ingredients here as in other Regency books. The denouement depends on the risk of losing reputation by breaking the social rules, a risk which gains its power through the very attractiveness of fashionable society despite – or, perhaps, because of – its frivolity. Hard work for a simple but comfortable life-style might be commended in the book but the story's very existence depends on the need to escape, at least in imagination, from such a condition.

The theme is, in any case, undercut by one of the principal incidents of the story: namely, that the hero's wealth is restored, not by being 'where the work's heaviest and hardest', but by the discovery of the hero's lost family jewels, and by hiding the fact that they have been found from the last owner's wife, who might also have had a claim to them in law. In other words, it is not honest toil, but chance and questionable honesty, which bring the wealth necessary for respect.

This is, of course, one of those sudden turns of fortune which are part of the very nature of romance and give it much of its wish-fulfilling power. Although the setting and the use of episodes like these show contemporary society to be very different from the kind of ideal economy described in the novel – based on chance rather than desert and encouraging a need to escape, if only for a few minutes in the imagination, from a life which frustrates aspiration rather than fulfils it – the romances use inequality of fortune to provide that escape and a surrogate fulfilment. The operation of chance seems to promise that everyone is in fact equal, and however far from the world of power and self-fulfilment our lives may seem, a turn of fortune's wheel might bring us into it. The fact that this world is made to seem so attractive suggests promise as well as surrogate satisfaction.

That the generic features of historical romance were still being used in the 1980s is testament to their power, even when the overt 'message' of the text seems to be directed at a 'modern' society whose members might be expected to sympathize with the idea of desert rather than with a resolution depending on the operation of chance.

*

Quality Maid is an earlier book than *Golden Barrier* (1973 as opposed to 1981), but the same preoccupation with deserved wealth, escape from poverty, and the contemptible nature of those who will not help themselves is there. These themes are, perhaps, less explicity stated than in the later book; by the 1980s when *Golden Barrier* was published, praise of competitiveness and hard work might have appeared more sympathetic, even in a romance. Like the later book, *Quality Maid* is set in the Regency period, and the 'quality' of the title defines the heroine from the beginning as upper-class. However, ill-fortune has robbed her family, the Longdens, of their wealth: the mother, who was the one with the money, having disappeared four years earlier leaving her money untouchable until she can be officially presumed dead. Since Mr Longden is blind and has lost all his money in an unfortunate speculation, the Longdens are almost starving.

The eldest daughter, Clemency, tries to persuade her rich neighbour, Piers, recently back from Australia, to help her find some sort of work. At first he is annoyed by this appeal for help. He had once been naïvely idealistic and had tried to help the unfortunate, just as Kate tries to help the tinkers in the later book. What had alerted him to the true nature of many of those he had tried to help – 'brash, idle, glib liars' (p.19) – was an attack upon him by a 'plausible rogue' of a convict he had assisted.

His sympathies are now reserved for those who live in 'primitive homes' in Australia, where he has been living, who are forced to employ 'women convicts' as servants (p.39). These home-owners are middle-class people who have gone to Australia, seeing it as a land of opportunity; life is hard, but they are willing to work in the knowledge that eventually they will gain wealth.

Clemency, who has dressed in her mother's clothes, looks very different from these paragons. Because the dress and hat are far too big for her she looks like a servant dressed up in her mistress's clothes to Piers, so that Clemency's effort to make herself look decent in fact makes her look ridiculously over-dressed and antagonizes him. He forces a kiss on her and it is only her reaction which makes him realize that in fact she is what she claims: 'Quality'. Later, a visit to the Longdens' house while they are having their meal reveals the pathetic truth: what little meat and vegetables they have goes to the blind father who eats them unaware that the girls are making do on a single potato shared between them.

Piers, now convinced that the Longdens are genuinely deserving of help, finds Clemency a job as his aunt's companion, but more and more he feels that he and she are linked by common interests and temperament. Clemency is fascinated by the details he relates of the wool business, and when he hurts his hand shows she has skills as a clerk by copying his accounts for him. The same pattern of events as in *Golden Barrier* is evident: Clemency wins her businessman husband, not because of her wealth and beauty but because she belongs to the same group of practical people as he does and is linked to the hero through their common interest in trade.

There is even a similar contrast between the deserving poor (the Longdens) and the undeserving. These are parasites upon society at best, and at worst dangerous elements within it – like the convict who attacks Piers. Pier's attitude towards the shiftless is further justified in the story by the career of the half-gypsy stable-boy, Will, to whom he refuses another chance after he has lost his job at the stable. Will has too much of his gypsy father in him – a 'smooth-tongued, cheating rascal' – and is not 'steady and reliable' (p.18). He goes off to join a gang of robbers, thus proving the rightness of Piers's assessment. In the end the robbers kidnap Clemency and hold her to ransom (she is in fact rescued by Piers and this brings the two together and precipitates the happy ending). In these circumstances, the lad's kindness towards Clemency wins him Piers's patronage, which turns him from a criminal to a loyal servant; and his new loyalty reinstates him in society as Piers's servant, firmly integrated into the social hierarchy instead of being an anarchic element on its periphery. His role is now akin to that of the tenants in *Golden Barrier*, who are grateful to Dermot for finding them work.

As in the later book, however, the setting and denouement contradict the impression given by the theme of the book. Piers is presented more as a country landowner who enjoys shooting on his estate than as a businessman, and not all the Longdens' good fortune comes from Clemency's hard work. Piers's aunt gives new clothes to all the girls – described in detail so that the reader can enjoy them – and introduces the youngest into local society. In addition, the girls decide to sell some of the family jewellery which is already in their possession; but the need to do so is removed by the happy chance of Mrs Longden's discovery: having lost her memory after a murderous attack by a highwayman, she is living in York.

Her fortune is now available to the family and they regain their lost place in society.

The status of the Longdens as 'quality' means that in this book there is less stress on new elements in society taking over from the decadent aristocracy. What is shocking about the way in which Piers treats Clemency is not that any woman should have kisses forced upon her, but that a lady should – even a poor one. The deserving characters belong to the middle or upper classes and the undeserving ones to the lower. There is more of an impression of a natural divide between upper and lower here than in the later book.

Both books, however, show similar contradictory elements. Both praise self-help and enterprise; both contain elements of good fortune. In *Quality Maid* the happy chance of finding the family jewels which features in *Golden Barrier* is matched by that of finding a lost wife: the interchangeability of jewels and wife as bringers of fortune being emphasized by the way Mrs Longden is simply substituted for jewels as a provider of money. Both jewels and woman function as a kind of Hitchcockian McGuffin, a device whose exact nature is unimportant, whose function in this case is to bring good fortune to the deserving characters in the story. The effect of this is to undermine the theme of the book very considerably.

*

These two books are by no means unusual, though. The features they display are shown by many similar romances from the 1970s and 1980s. The inevitable contradictions may, however, have suggested to some writers and readers the unsuitability of the romantic form for this particular economic message. The new forms of popular historical fiction - and, in particular, the saga, a form which has gained prominence in the 1970s and 1980s – may perhaps owe their growth in popularity to this factor. Robert Hewison reviewed a number of books belonging to such saga sequences in an article in the *Times Literary Supplement* of 28 August 1981.[7] The pleasure they offered, he thought, related to what he called a celebration of 'getting on'. He felt they showed an ambivalence towards industrial society, rejecting it by retreating to a past time in which its effects were less noticeable, while at the same time showing sympathy with the capitalistic individualism which accompanied, and to a certain extent produced, the Industrial Revolution. This is certainly the kind of feeling which one can find in the work of Mira Stables and other contemporary writers.

In practice, however much praise is heaped upon hard work and natural desert, the actual distribution of reward in the story typically comes about through the medium of chance. Scenes of work are especially rare in the stories; the characteristic denouement depends instead on an unexpected inheritance, the finding of a lost treasure, or a piece of good fortune at the gaming tables.

In Eva Macdonald's *House of Secrets* (1980), for instance, it is not the independent spirit of the heroine which brings her first a modest fortune and then a rich marriage, but a chance meeting with a man who likes her well enough to leave her his tea-shop and the location of a hidden lode of silver. In the same way, the hero of *Highwayman's Hazard* (1983) by Marina Oliver regains his father's fortune not because of his right to it, though he has one, but because of his skill at cards which enables him to beat his enemy at a game of Hazard. Dorothy Dunnett's hero, Lymond, in *The Game of Kings* (1962) is proved innocent through his pupil's skill and good fortune at tarocco, a game of chance based on the tarot pack. Instances could be cited almost indefinitely: this is one of the most frequent motifs in the genre. Yet the skills of Hazard and the other games are scarcely to be promoted in a just society, and, in any case, most of the games rely as much upon chance as upon skill.

The result is that however much romantic authors might seek to fit the message of the text to the dominant attitudes of the time, the generic features of romance are too enduring to allow of an uncomplicated statement of them. The way in which 'desert' as a theme is constantly subverted by the element of chance in the story is symptomatic of this; readers still demand the wish-fulfilling motifs of romance, and this seems to suggest that, ironically, the more the writers proclaim a just society the more their readers demand escape from its constraints.

Chapter 7

'Brute heroes' and 'spirited heroines'

Women's historical romance, as developed by Georgette Heyer in the 1920s, and by her innumerable followers from the 1930s to the present, uses the past setting and the stock motifs of romance for a new purpose: the symbolic expression of female concerns, a function which the genre, with its blend of fantasy and the 'credibility' of a historical setting, was well suited to fulfil.

Women's romance has been the subject of a certain amount of critical attention in the last decade. The fact that its features are very marked has raised questions about the kinds of pleasure women readers derive from such texts, with their apparently unpleasant images of male dominance and female submission. Feminist critics in particular have been divided in their interpretation of the generic situations, some seeing them as subverting the attitudes of a patriarchal society, others as confirming them. Where Germaine Greer, for example, has stated that in 'inventing' the typically brutal hero of romance, women are 'cherishing the chains of their bondage',[1] Tania Modleski believes, first, that women did not 'invent' masculine characters who 'assert masculine superiority in the same ways men often do in real life',[2] and, second, that the pleasure of a romantic text comes for women in large part 'from the elements of a revenge fantasy, from our conviction that the woman is bringing the man to his knees'.[3]

Modleski rejects the reading which sees in the romances a 'Freudian paradigm of the young girl's maturation process', through which girls can be seen 'learning to forego identification with the male', to see him instead as an object of 'erotic attachment',[4] because such a 'maturation' comes about only through an infantile fantasy – the heroine putting herself in danger so that the hero will suffer from her loss.

Tony Bennett and Janet Woollacott suggest that the 'phallic castration of the hero' which, like Modleski, they find in the typical romance ('the wounding, mutilation or blinding of the hero'[5] – not *physical* castration, though, for, as Modleski points out, the hero needs to retain his potency or the revenge will not achieve its object) allows the heroine not vengeance but an opportunity to take the male role. While both Modleski and Bennett and Woollacott see some element of a vengeance fantasy in the novels, Janice Radway considers them to be chiefly about 'transformation': the hero is 'feminized', developing qualities of 'motherly' tenderness and care already latent in his nature.[6]

All these critics consider the novels from the viewpoint of the woman reader's experience: the peculiar nature of the novels is considered to arise from the fact that they are addressed to women readers. Modleski, for instance, sees her work as a contribution to 'a psychology of the interaction between feminine readers and texts. Analyzing Harlequins, Gothics and soap operas seems a good way to begin . . . because the works are aimed predominantly or exclusively at a female audience.'[7] Although this does not necessarily imply that such texts are produced primarily *by* women, the defence of the 'woman writer' associated with the defence of female texts[8] implies a supposition that the Harlequins and Gothics at least are, especially since Modleski traces the genre back through the sentimental novel and the domestic novel, both often written by women, to Charlotte Brontë and Jane Austen.[9]

Women's historical romance, however, has close links with the adventure stories of writers such as Weyman, Conan Doyle, Orczy and Sabatini, which are mainly centred around the experience of the hero and give every sign of being aimed primarily at men, even if they attracted a general readership. The two kinds of historical romance share a number of common motifs, and while the adventure stories contain some love interest, the female romances usually include some element of adventure or suspense as well. Moreover, at least one of the earlier writers, Stanley Weyman, used the English Regency setting so popular in female romance for some of his novels, such as *The Castle Inn* (1898) and *Starvecrow Farm* (1905), and in these books the situations are uncannily close to the formula for female historical romance developed by Heyer and her followers.

This raises the question of the significance of these situations, since it seems unlikely that a masculine-orientated text by a male

writer would contain the same messages about gender as those by
and for women. I should like, therefore, to examine the various
possible interpretations of the formulaic situations as produced by
both men and women by comparing three novels: Weyman's
Starvecrow Farm, Heyer's *Regency Buck* (1935), and a novel by a
present-day writer, Rowena Tenet's *Bewitching Imposter* (1983).

*

A description of the basic situation of *Starvecrow Farm* gives an
impression of a typical male-centred story, very like Weyman's
usual output. Set in the aftermath of the Cato Street conspiracy of
1820 – a plan to assassinate the Cabinet – the novel deals with the
escape abroad of some of the conspirators, aided by the kidnapping
of the son of a Lancashire magistrate. The magistrate, Captain
Clyne, is notorious for his harsh justice: to the radical Walterson he
is not only a man who can 'transport a man for seven years for
poaching a hare' (p.8), but as a naval captain had been suspected of
'flogging a man to death' (p.8), and it is also possible that he gave the
order to the troops to ride down the demonstrators at Peterloo.
Weyman's authorial comments on Clyne, however, present him in a
more attractive light, more like the justice-loving des Ageaux in *The
Abbess of Vlaye*; 'It was his honest belief that a little severity – in
other words, a whiff of the grape-shot – would have nipped the
French Revolution in the bud' (p.61). He is severe, in other words,
because he believes it will help to maintain the stability of society,
which would benefit everyone.

Clyne thus not only resembles other heroes in Weyman's novels;
he also represents the forces of law and order ranged against radical
anarchy – a favourite theme of Weyman's. Situation and character
in the novel link it with other 'masculine' novels by the same author.
What makes it unusual is that it is told, not, as one might expect,
from Clyne's viewpoint but from that of his cousin Henrietta, who
first hinders him and then becomes his ally in the search for his
abducted son. It is her experiences which provide the story-line, and
Clyne first appears in the story not as a magistrate but as the suitor
from whom she is fleeing. One of the main lines of plot-interest is the
way in which the hostility between the two changes to love as Clyne
comes to recognize Henrietta's worth and Henrietta learns to
subordinate her desire for autonomy to his will.

Despite its masculine features, therefore, the experience of
reading this novel is very like that of reading one of the female-

centred romances of Heyer or Cartland, or one of the Harlequin romances which Modleski describes; it follows a similar pattern to the Harlequin formula:

> a young, inexperienced, poor to moderately well-to-do woman encounters and becomes involved with a handsome, strong, experienced, wealthy man, older than herself by ten to fifteen years. The heroine is confused by the hero's behaviour since, though he is obviously interested in her, he is mocking, cynical, contemptuous, often hostile and even somewhat brutal. By the end, however, all misunderstandings are cleared away, and the hero reveals his love for the heroine, who reciprocates.[10]

Clyne is certainly older than Henrietta; he has retired from the sea and is a widower with a little boy. Like the Harlequin heroes he is hostile and 'even somewhat brutal' to Henrietta throughout much of the story. At their first meeting in the book, after she has eloped from home with Walterson – one of the conspirators in disguise – he tells her brusquely that her family has cast her off and that he is also breaking off their engagement. He tells her that his chaplain is willing to marry her out of charity and suggests that she takes up the offer.

Like many a later heroine in search of independence (a form of Modleski's 'identification with the male'), she is outraged at this casual disposal of her, and refuses angrily. Paradoxically, her defiance rouses Clyne's interest for the first time, and he at least pledges bail for her so that she is free to walk about the countryside. Later, however, he comes to believe that she knows where Walterson, who has abandoned her and is in hiding, is – and, more importantly, where he is keeping his son. He tries to bully her into telling him Walterson's whereabouts. Henrietta, curiously, is roused and excited by his violence rather than frightened, though she feels humiliated and angry at the same time and refuses to tell him anything. The language in which this episode is described has a certain erotic charge, like the descriptions of male dominance in female-centred romance: 'he had seized her wrist, gripping it cruelly', so that Henrietta feels it be a 'humiliation' (p.176-7); but it is apparent when they talk later that she has pleasurable memories of the episode. It seems that, after marriage, Clyne will dominate and Henrietta will enjoy it.

Her reaction seems to fit in with Germaine Greer's comment on male dominance, quoted above (see p.107), as 'cherishing the chains of their bondage'. The outcome, however, suggests rather that this is one of the stages which Modleski maps out for romantic heroines ('The heroines rebel against the male authority figure . . . but then comes the constant reminder of the impossibility of winning . . . if you can't lick them, you might as well love them').[11]

Certainly, the episode seems to spell the end of Henrietta's rebellion and the beginning of womanliness. Henrietta is conquered – partly, perhaps, because of a new feeling for Clyne aroused by his action, partly by Clyne's love for his son, which rouses her latent motherly feelings; as a result she is haunted with pity for the little boy, and later puts herself in danger to help Clyne find and rescue him. Just as Modleski's heroes discover the heroine's 'infinite preciousness' because of the threats to her life, so the danger to Henrietta makes Clyne realize the nature of his feelings for her. He is forced, in declaring his love for her, to acknowledge his misjudgement of her, so that the blend of 'childish fantasy' and 'revenge' which Modleski sees at the heart of female romance is to be found in this book too.

In this case, however, it is unlikely that the author was expressing any such fantasy, or that his male readers were excited by the thought of female revenge. Any eroticism to be found in the bullying scene might in fact come from 'the ideology of rape' mentioned by Susan Brownmiller,[12] who suggests that female romance provides a mirror-image of male fantasy – female fantasy being necessarily conditioned by the dominant male ideology. The 'logic' of the ideology seems to be that violence and a will to dominate are natural in men, especially in sexual relationships, and women themselves respond to them, even, at times, provoking them. Such an ideology certainly seems to inform the assumptions upon which this and other novels of Weyman – A Gentleman of France contains a similar motif – are based. On the other hand, the heroes of romance may show themselves tempted to commit rape, but the sign of their heroism is their abstention: Clyne shows himself to be chivalric and protective, as an Edwardian gentleman should be, and so a worthy husband for Henrietta.

Henrietta herself is like later heroines in being both self-assertive and childish. She is described at the beginning of the novel (p.9) as having 'much folly' and 'vast ignorance' and 'her childishness, her frivolity, her naïveté' are referred to. She has eloped with Walterson not because she loves him or shares his radical views but because 'the only liberty in which he had been able to interest her had been her own' (p.8). The context makes it clear that she was looking for a freedom she knew she would never find in the 'unlovely marriage' (p.2) planned for her with Clyne, who merely sees her as a convenience, 'a mother for your child', as she tells him (p.74). Her speculation sounds as if it is one of the 'false clues' which Modleski argues are 'explanations for the contempt men show towards women':[13] she quotes from one of the Harlequin romances a very similar paragraph: 'men, in her experience, took a woman because she was convenient and a good worker'.[14]

In *Starvecrow Farm*, however, Clyne really *does* despise Henrietta; unlike the heroes of the Harlequins, he had not assumed a mask for a secret sexual attraction. What is more, the text seems to suggest that he was right to despise her; no heroine of a woman's romance was ever described in such derogatory terms. Henrietta is to be condemned, and her condemnation can be traced to the ideology of the text. The implication is that women who behave as she has behaved deserve to be made outlaws, not because of any evil intent but because women should not try to be free. The text makes clear in any case that what Henrietta wants, deep inside herself, is not more freedom but love and tenderness: in eloping with Walterson she was really running away from a 'cold home', an 'unfeeling sister-in-law' and a brother who hunted all day and was drunk all night (p.2). This is what redeems her as a heroine; a woman who wants love is a sympathetic figure, and even her feeling for Walterson is understandable – she thinks of him as someone who will take care of her: 'she had cast away every stay but his' (p.9).

Henrietta's portrayal is in accord with the concept of woman as 'the angel in the house': pure and innocent, but with that innocence forever menaced by the taint of the world. Her purity therefore depends upon her remaining within the narrow limits allotted to good women by society, as she finds out. Having made her bid for liberty, it is clear that she has stepped outside the circle of protection which surrounds middle-class women. At first, she does not understand the implications of this, but it is soon apparent that she has crossed the divide which separates one kind of woman – a lady, to be treated with respect and protected by men – from another: one who is freer to act according to her own judgement, but in return lays herself open to every kind of insult and ill-treatment.

The first sign of this is when the magistrate (called, with perhaps unconscious appropriateness, Hornyold) questions her about Walterson's whereabouts. He uses a 'familiar tone' which no one has ever used to her before, calls her patronizingly 'my girl' and thinks her 'no better than the imprudent wenches the overseers were continually bringing before him' (p.49), as though imprudence were not only socially levelling but, more to the point, morally dubious and perhaps actually criminal as well.

Impressions of vulnerability are strongly reinforced. Henrietta is cast off by her family who feel she is a 'disgrace' to them (p.74). Hornyold, the magistrate, makes a pass at her as she walks along a footpath, believing that a woman in her position must be 'no better than she should be'. Later, she is nearly raped by a gypsy and has to be saved by Clyne and his chaplain.

The very harmlessness of her behaviour – all she has really done is to spend a night away from home, and she actually takes the precaution of putting herself under the landlady's protection when she reaches the inn, so there can be no question of sexual immorality – is stressed as much as her punishment. The offensiveness of the magistrate, the law officers and, to a lesser extent, Clyne and her own family, is based on misconceptions, and this is the basis of her later imprisonment for her refusal to say where Walterson is.

The point is made, however, that this is what can happen once a young woman steps outside what is normally expected of her. She does not need to be immoral to be persecuted: to be female, and alone, is enough. A symbol of her helplessness can be seen when she is sent to prison under suspicion of being an accessory to Walterson's escape, in her inability to lock her cell door to keep herself from being molested: she must be locked in by the gaoler or not at all. In her own life, she no sooner tries to take control of her fate than she comes to grief.

Weyman presents her, therefore, as a woman who is not bad in herself, but who is ill-advised in trying to combat the inevitable limitations of being a woman, since the forces of society are too strong for her – or rather, as a woman, she is too weak to resist them. In any case, they are there for her protection in a brutish world. Liberty of action is quite literally impossible for a lady, since to seek it is to lose the right to that status. What happens to Henrietta is symbolic of this impossibility: the only result of her bid for freedom is more constraint. Throughout the book, the heroine, in search of a wider freedom, has moved from one prison to another narrower one as she breaks the social shibboleths. From being locked into her room at the inn, she is taken to the Kendal gaol, and in the climactic episode of the novel endures the claustrophobic horror of the smuggler's oven, a coffin-like aperture cut out of the rock which had been used to store contraband articles in the disreputable past of Starvecrow farm, and where the radical gang imprison Henrietta and Clyne's son. Though escape supposedly brings her freedom, it is physical freedom only; in the description of her life after she is married to Clyne the prison is seen as internalized in phrases such as 'caged her wildness and tamed her pride' (p.314) – which are the words used to describe the result of Henrietta's marriage and motherhood.

Although the prison image is presumably a way of showing the naturalness and inevitability of the limitations upon the role of Edwardian middle-class women, the impression it gives is not a happy one; the use of so ominous a symbol is one of those significant slips which makes it seem as though the unconscious of the text harbours a different interpretation, one less favourable to the attitudes of contemporary society. Elaine Showalter has commented upon the ways in which a feminist reading of a text can so alter its interpretation that the plot itself seems to be radically changed:

> In the purest feminist literary criticism we are . . . presented with a radical alteration of our vision, a demand that we see meaning in what has previously been empty space. The orthodox plot recedes, and another plot . . . stands out in bold relief like a thumbprint.[15]

Pierre Macherey has argued that the resolution of conflicts in a fictional text provides an 'imagined order', impossible to achieve in real life: a 'resolution so precarious that it is obvious in the very letter of the text where incoherence and incompleteness burst forth'.[16] The unhappy choice of symbol can be seen as just such a 'defect of the text': one which leads the reader to an apprehension of 'new truth' as long as they are alert to the contradiction. Weyman's novel may therefore be seen as confirming an Edwardian male view of gender in society; but cues in the text show that the same situations can actually be used to subvert this view.

It may be argued, therefore, that this is why the very features which were used in Weyman's novels and others of the same period to build a picture of a society where masculine qualities were dominant became so compelling to women readers later in the century, when the fashion for masculine adventure stories had passed. For women, these features could express a degree of dissent

– though what degree may be seen from an analysis of a female novel.

*

Starvecrow Farm was published in 1905, two years after the formation of the Women's Social and Political Union, at a time when suffragette agitation was becoming an important public issue. In the thirty years between its publication and that of Georgette Heyer's *Regency Buck* (1935), women had gained the vote (although it was at first a limited form of the franchise: full adult suffrage for women had been granted only in 1928, seven years before Heyer published her novel),[17] and had had the experience of performing 'men's' jobs during the war. By 1918 'well over a million women' had entered, for the first time, 'upon paid, and usually arduous, tasks': as bus conductresses, porters, munitions workers, office clerks, the services and the auxiliary police, for example.[18] The inter-war years saw other changes in women's position: the 1920s was the decade of the 'bright young things', bringing new, 'boyish' styles of dress for women and an 'emancipation' which included 'open indulgence in drink, tobacco and cosmetics . . . insistence on smaller families . . . easier facilities for divorce'.[19]

David Thomson has pointed out, however, that many of the new freedoms affected only a small number of women, the majority adopting new styles of dress and freedom of manners, but with traditional roles remaining essentially untouched.[20] The continuing problem of unemployment, for example, meant that a good deal of resentment was felt against working women and pressure was put on them to return to the home.[21] Though C. L. Mowatt points to changes in sexual morality – 'people were continuously "popping" in and out of bed with new bed-fellows'[22] – the more extreme changes were confined to the small and exclusive group about which Evelyn Waugh and Noël Coward wrote.[23] None the less, one might have expected the new freedoms, however limited in practice, to have made some impact on attitudes, however slight.

If they did, it is not reflected in *Regency Buck*, written in 1935. There are noticeable parallels between the two texts: the situation at the beginning of *Regency Buck*, with the heroine moving outside the narrow behavioural limits allowed her and suffering abuse as a result, is virtually the same as that of Henrietta in *Starvecrow Farm*. Like Henrietta, the heroine has to learn to subordinate her will to that of an authoritarian male, for whom she first feels dislike but later comes to love.

The most striking difference between the two books is that *Regency Buck* lacks the political dimension of *Starvecrow Farm* – the confrontation between magistrate and radicals which sets the plot in motion. This has the effect of foregrounding the situation of women and offering it for exploration. The readership for Heyer's romances was by this time mainly female,[24] and such an exploration may have been particularly appealing at this time because women's experiences during the war may have aroused a more widespread consciousness of the actual limitations of their lives. More probably, perhaps, the readers of Heyer's novels were aware of changes in women's position and in sexual behaviour but did not necessarily like them. The historical setting allowed a return in imagination to a time when sexual morality was strict and gender roles clearly defined; if the actualities of Regency society were different, Heyer had invented a society which seemed to be like this. The respondents to the survey carried out in 1974 by Peter Mann for Mills & Boon,[25] many of whom were old enough to have read *Regency Buck* when it was first published, mentioned that the appeal of romance was that it was 'clean' and the heroines 'decent'.[26]

There are differences in the ideology of gender between the two books, however. If *Starvecrow Farm* showed women to be subordinate, it also showed them to be 'better' than men, though only as long as they remain within the limitations imposed by society. Men are concerned with the world of affairs, but there is more than a suggestion in *Starvecrow Farm* that they would be better if they had more understanding of matters within the 'feminine' realm, such as feelings and relationships. If Henrietta has to learn to accept Clyne's authority, Clyne has to learn to respect her as a person – she complains that he has never offered her love during their engagement and has made it clear that he considers her a mere convenience (p.94).

Men are shown as learning to respect and understand the feminine world in other romances by Weyman, such as *Under the Red Robe*.[27] Feminine qualities are necessary to civilization, but the feminine world of purity and innocence, where loyalty and personal relationships are important, is a fragile one, constantly menaced by masculine aggression, as both Weyman and A. E. W. Mason show. Hence the importance of chivalry in the books of the 1890s and

1900s: a good man controlled aggressive impulses in himself and protected women from those in others. This is not quite the picture presented in *Regency Buck*, although some of the differences can be attributed to a change to a female viewpoint. Heyer frequently opposes 'nature' to 'society' when presenting women's behaviour, as though questioning how far the 'realities' of gender which are taken for granted in the male-centred romances *are* in fact natural. Although, like Weyman, Heyer shows women's freedom of movement as circumscribed by their weakness in the face of masculine violence and insult, the situations of the novel throw into higher relief the unfairness of this; the way Regency society is presented as stressing the importance of female innocence as an essential commodity in the marriage market gives a good opportunity for this. Fears of masculine aggression and doubts about masculine trustworthiness – a theme central to present-day Gothic romance according to Joanna Russ[28] – are also expressed in Heyer's work, although here there is an element of continuity with Weyman: Henrietta's similar doubts about Walterson are made clear in the first few pages of *Starvecrow Farm*, and in such a way as to suggest that she automatically sees herself as dependent upon him.

In Heyer's work, the construction of the hero as autocratic and often rude and ill-mannered – the brutal hero who was to become the hallmark of women's romance, with an ancestry reaching back through Charlotte Brontë's Rochester to the Byronic hero, with some influence from Jane Austen's Darcy – allowed for the exploration of such fears. The construction of heroines who were themselves strong-willed and who gave an impression of un-developed potential allowed an opportunity for the expression of a female need for self-development which is not met by the pa-triarchal society of Heyer's novels. An admission of the validity of the female wish to meet this need is something not found in the male-centred novels; either changing attitudes or the female view-point made it possible for female novelists to express it.

*

The story of *Regency Buck* is that of Judith Taverner, a wealthy heiress, whose riches, together with her country upbringing in Yorkshire, have given her a strong will, a sense of independence and a natural directness of behaviour which shows her ignorance of the rules of polite society. This means that she embodies the 'natural' qualities which are often associated with the heroines of Heyer's romances - Léonie in *These Old Shades*, for instance, is presented as opposing her love of natural behaviour to the social restrictions prescribed by her guardian's sister, Lady Fanny, a situation epitomized in her protest about exchanging the boy's breeches she has been wearing for a lady's petticoats: as she is laced into her gown she protests 'something will burst . . . Me, perhaps'(p.119).

This implication that conforming to social norms necessitates a destruction of the self for women is relevant to *Regency Buck* as well: Judith has to be socialized out of her 'Yorkshire' behaviour. Her lack of knowledge of the rules of polite society may seem less likely than Léonie's ignorance, since Léonie had been brought up as a boy in a Paris tavern, whereas Judith's upbringing has been that of a lady; but a 'Yorkshire' upbringing is used as an excuse for lack of social knowledge in other books by Heyer, such as *Arabella* (1940). Presumably Yorkshire seemed far enough away from London to make such ignorance credible, given the slowness of travel by carriage.

Judith's sense of independence and strength of will can be seen as taking the place of Léonie's freedom of action as a 'boy'; they give her a strong sense of selfhood which must be modified if she is to be fully socialized. This is evident from the beginning of the book, when she is first introduced, travelling to London with her young brother Peregrine for the Season, to which she is looking forward as both enjoyable in itself and a gateway into the fuller, freer, adult world – that is, a world which will give her more independence, not less.

These expectations are rapidly frustrated. In Grantham, she finds herself delayed because all the post horses have been hired out to gentlemen who have flocked to the town to see a prize-fight. The fight is an emblem of masculine aggressiveness very alien to her feminine world, and she shows her ignorance of the implications – that the town will be full of men, away from their families and out for a good time, so that it will also have become a magnet for prostitutes and *demi-mondaines*, and there will be a general laxity of behaviour – by going for a country walk on her own and even taking off her sandal to shake out a stone. Her behaviour is *natural*, but breaks the social rules and is, by implication, provocative. As in *Starvecrow Farm* the essential innocence (and, indeed, in this instance, triviality) of the heroine's action is foregrounded, as though to stress female vulnerability and the impossibility of a woman's situation. A passing gentleman on his way to the fight mistakes her for a village girl and steals a kiss.

There are, of course, implications about class attitudes in this 'stolen kiss' motif, which is found frequently in Heyer's work and other female romances. The lower classes, it is implied, are fair game for the wealthy. That this has enough foundation in reality to pass without examination is suggested by the way in which female servants were often abused by their masters. According to Joy Melville, 'the wealthy had complete power over their domestic servants',[29] and she quotes the case of a girl who, made pregnant by the master who had raped her, was 'faced with the workhouse'. For some, if they were under age, the local asylum waited, under the provision of the Mental Health Act of 1913.[30]

The Grantham 'gentleman's' behaviour aligns him with Weyman's Hornyold as one who both enforces (on the victims) and abuses the laws which are supposed to protect women. When Judith arrives in London she meets the gentleman in a more formal context when she calls upon her guardian, the Earl of Worth, and finds him to be the very man who had molested her. In this role he enforces an absolute correctness of behaviour upon her – a correctness made necessary by the behaviour of men like him, as he blandly admits when he warns her against staying in towns where prize-fights are being held. Judith is indignant at his injustice, but he is amused, accepting the injustice of the situation which allows sexual licence to the male but not to the female. He has, in any case, in his dual role as predator and protector, an absolute social power over her which he can use just as he pleases.

His position as Judith's guardian gives him an intimate connection with those rules of propriety by which she must live as long as she remains in society. As he falls in love with her, he also becomes a potential consumer of Judith's combination of virtue and sexuality and therefore has a double interest in building fences around her behaviour.

This 'propriety' is the central concept of many Heyer books; it highlights the economic base of the notion of purity with which the romances concern themselves. The purity of the female is necessary for family property to pass down an undisputed line of descent from father to son. Female purity therefore has an economic importance in a patriarchal society, supporting male wealth and power through restricting the woman's life. Heyer's comments show how clearly this was seen and resented by her heroines, and her books and succeeding texts make clear that the whole apparatus of London society was set up to provide those restrictions until marriageable girls (with suitable heredity and wealth) were safely married off.

The rules themselves may be viewed as constricting, but they are fascinating as well: they offer an induction into a society whose attractions are one of the main wish-fulfilment elements in the books. By entering it, the heroine puts off the limitations of childhood and takes up her adult role. The paradox by which, in doing so, she gains more independence and less ability to enjoy it, is solved by a number of factors, the most important of which is romantic love, seen more as a 'magical' resolution of an impossible situation than as a feeling to be explored for its own sake.

Judith's growing awareness of the rules of polite society is one of the main themes of *Regency Buck* and brings out their attractions. The prestige of Almacks, the rooms where young society girls go to dance and meet suitable young men, depends to some extent on the difficulty of obtaining vouchers for the dances and the need for absolute propriety of conduct to deserve them. They are in the gift of a group of Patronesses who, like Avon's cousin Harriet or Weyman's Mrs Gilson, can be seen as the actual enforcers of the rules which ultimately derive from male needs.

Judith is fascinated by the rules, annoyed by the constraints they impose, and eager both to learn and to challenge them, to see how far she can go in asserting her personal freedom without sacrificing propriety. In this she has no less a person than Beau Brummel as her mentor. He tells her what things she may do, and be accepted as merely eccentric, and what things she may not do, on pain of expulsion from society. The climactic episode involves a confrontation between her and the masterful hero, who is also her guardian (as, of course, Avon was Léonie's).

Judith is driving herself down to Brighton in an open carriage – a phaeton, which is in any case a 'daring' carriage for a lady. The hero stops her, to point out that to be seen driving on such a busy road is beyond the permitted limits of female behaviour: she may be seen and ogled by all the young bucks who drive to Brighton in their turn. She has allowed self-will, he tells her, to lead her 'into a scrape which might, were I not here to enforce your obedience to my commands, have damaged your reputation more seriously than you know . . . you have been grossly at fault' (p.230).

Up to this point, the contest between them has seemed an equal one between two strong-willed people. This statement, however, shows this to be illusion. Judith does not question Worth's right to censure her conduct in this way for long. His attitude is undeniably unfair; his previous behaviour still rankles. Women are expected to be guardians of morality both against and on behalf of men; the story brings out the unfairness of this very clearly. None the less, they accept tacitly the unfairness: Judith admits that 'There could be no defending her conduct' (p.230). She seems with this thought to have internalized the masculine system of values and taken it for her own – something which most of Heyer's heroines do at some point in her novels.

The rules therefore seem to ensure the maintenance of a female role which is limited by the needs of monogamy in a society informed by a double standard of morality, male sexual adventures being implicitly licensed whereas complete chastity is necessary for unmarried females. Though Almacks and the rest of the meeting places form a 'marriage market', so that it is important for the women to go about in public and be seen there, their behaviour outside the home is carefully regulated.

Thus, at Almacks, waltzing, which permits physical contact between men and women, is strictly controlled: a girl may only waltz if she has been introduced to a partner expressly for that purpose by one of the Patronesses. A female may not go down St James's Street, where the gentleman's clubs are, since even the sight of a girl by men must be strictly limited: the reason usually given, like Worth's for Judith's not driving down the Brighton Road, is that she will be subject to 'insult' from masculine ogling. This is much more extreme than the limitations in *Starvecrow Farm* and suggests almost a 'purdah' situation; even to be seen is potentially contaminating. The importance of the 'male look' which constructs the female as a passive source of erotic pleasure has been noted by Mulvey,[31] and the stress on this custom in Heyer suggests a female protest at being constructed in such terms: Heyer's more spirited heroines, like Judith or the eponymous heroine of *The Grand Sophy* (1950), refuse to have their movements confined by fear of the look because they feel that there is more to them than to be the central figure in a male sexual fantasy.

Clothes, too, must be cut according to the fashion, which at once conceals and displays the female form. The loose, high-waisted dresses of the Regency suggest in any case an innocent and natural girlishness; but if a girl wishes to look more natural – in fact, almost 'naked' – by damping her petticoat, she is thought sadly 'fast'. The action forms the boundary between the innocent naturalness and challenge of the heroine and the over-boldness of women of the world who take their pleasures like a man.

Judith learns to accept the picture of femininity as subject to taint by the very existence of masculinity around her. The notion is reminiscent of Mason's picture of Countess Lukstein standing asleep and clothed in white while her husband's blood flows towards her to stain her robe.[32] None the less, there is a difference in attitude. Mason's and Weyman's books suggested that the feminine realm had its own important but fragile value. Heyer's books suggest that women need to protect their 'purity' because it is a commodity, but that in a fair society they should not have to. In discussing the rules the books draw attention to the absurd limitations they impose on women's activity, so that the description itself is the grounds for an implied 'feminine protest'. But in accepting so blatantly unfair a situation, Judith is tacitly acknowledging that, however unfair a patriarchal society may be, it is one which brings a woman true fulfilment.

This fulfilment is, of course, through romantic love. The love-match allows a woman the protection she needs to gain some kind of freedom without putting herself in jeopardy from masculine aggressiveness, and it also allows her a relationship in which she can be valued for herself and not as a commodity (as in the 'marriage of convenience'). This is the prison which Henrietta entered willingly at the end of *Starvecrow Farm*, and it is what Judith eventually finds she wants more than individual freedom.

Love is seen in Heyer's work as a matter of affinity, rather than of physical attraction, though this is an element in it. Worth kisses Judith at the beginning of *Regency Buck* as a sign of casual attraction; the halt which his guardianship of her imposes on his courtship allows him time to come to value her as nearly an equal, well able to handle all kinds of social situations and possessed of a will almost as strong as his own. Physical love is therefore seen as a crowning expression of this value for each other's individual qualities, rather than as an end in itself.

The rules of society play their part in developing this value for each other in hero and heroine, since it is by her attitude towards them that the heroine commonly demonstrates her individual qualities. Although, clearly, Heyer could not always use the expedient of putting her heroine into boy's clothes in order to give her a 'masculine' freedom of action and strength of personality, her later heroines tended to be like Léonie – the heroine of *These Old Shades* who spent years masquerading as a boy – in being more natural in their attitudes than the majority of débutantes, and usually marked out by other unusual personality traits – strength of will, or intelligence and humour, or warmth of heart, for example. All these qualities are notable in Judith. Because she has a strong character, she comes into conflict early in the romance with the dominant personality of the hero, and so the two come to know and, eventually, to value each other's qualities. The function of the plot is to provide opportunities for them to do so.

At the end of the book Judith, however strong-willed and rebellious she may have seemed, implicitly affirms the 'natural' authority of Worth by forgetting all his outrages and falling into his arms. The unfairness remains: that is obvious. Love, it is implied, resolves all problems.

Heyer's work contains little of that description of rhapsodic feeling so common in Barbara Cartland's work. Rather, love is presented as an admission of care: Worth is always at hand to rescue Judith from those situations he is not himself responsible for. As Modleski has suggested, the hero has to admit at some point in the narrative that the heroine has become of central importance in his life, and that this importance springs only in part from sexual feeling. 'Love' in Heyer's books is a complete acceptance of the other person and a delight in their personal qualities. In also taking responsibility for the heroine's welfare, the hero demonstrates those 'feminine' qualities which are represented by the 'chivalry' of heroes of the older romances; while, for the heroine, to be recognized and valued by a powerful, charismatic individual is presented as so desirable that it compensates easily for the unfairness and injustice of society. This is the element of 'infantile regression' which Modleski finds in such resolutions, or Janice Radway's search for the mother:[33] that the heroine's self-image is created not by the woman herself but is the creation of a male authority figure.

*

Heyer's romances provided a pattern for later historical romances for women. It might be expected that, over half a century since Heyer began writing (in 1921 with *The Black Moth*), contemporary romances would show many changes, but it is a testimony to the strength of continuity within the genre and, perhaps, to a lack of any essential change in attitudes towards women, that the differences between Heyer's *Regency Buck* of 1935 and a romance of the 1980s are in fact very small. In Rowena Tenet's *Bewitching Imposter* (1983) many of the features of Heyer's romances are evident: the 'natural' heroine who has within her a potential for becoming more than a subordinate female, but who accepts limitations upon her personality and her role partly through love and partly through socialization; a hero whose masculinity poses a threat to the heroine, but who learns to develop the more caring side which links him to femininity; and a sense that the feminine realm is in some ways 'better' than the harsh male world, but so fragile it can only exist either in secrecy or through the permission and with the protection of the male. In this, it shows links not only with Heyer but with Weyman and other earlier romancers as well.

Bewitching Imposter is a novel which is closer to the 'bodice-ripper' than most of the contemporary romances surveyed in this book, but it has many of the features of the Heyer tradition; in fact, it demonstrates extreme forms of some of the romantic stereotypes, coming close at times to an actual send-up of the genre – as when the heroine's double, whose place she is to take in a royal marriage, turns out not only to be having an affair with someone else (a motif to be found in other books, such as Barbara Cartland's *Love Leaves at Midnight*, 1978), but to be pregnant by her lover with twins.

Thus, Shauna is an almost exaggeratedly 'natural' heroine, having been brought up in a remote Irish castle (Ireland is a signifier for 'naturalness' in other romances – such as Patricia Ormsby's *Joanna*, of 1977, in which the heroine is threatened with the disclosure of her innocent but free behaviour in her Irish home – in the same way as Heyer's 'Yorkshire'). Shauna has run 'barefoot and free' (p.14) from the wild marshes of her Irish childhood to be 'brought out' by her aunt in the stiff artificiality of London, and challenges not only the artificial rules of high society but those normal in any city – as, for instance, when she demonstrates to a group of interested young men in her aunt's drawing room how she got a pig out of the castle pantry. She is too innocent to realize that their interest comes from the fact that the demonstration involves a good deal of pulling up of skirts and revelation of ankles, and might not care if she did: like other heroines she resents the advice of her elders to act with more caution, refusing to limit her freedom because men see her primarily as a source of erotic pleasure. The aunt and uncle who are bringing Shauna out have been invited to the wedding of a minor member of European royalty, Alexis, Prince of Hanaria, to Ilena,

Princess of Tusshar. The marriage is very much a matter of state politics: this is the early nineteenth century, and it is feared that unless the small semi-Balkan states of Hanaria and Tusshar are seen to be united, they will disappear within Bonaparte's sphere of influence. Shauna's uncle is concerned about this danger, as a British diplomat who wishes to preserve Hanarian/Tussharian independence in Britain's interest, as a buffer against the power of Napoleon.

Ilena, however, is pregnant after a love affair with another neighbouring prince; and to avoid admitting this she is sent off into hiding, and Shauna, who happens to look exactly like her, takes her place on the insistence of Tussharian councillors who tell her that unless she complies her cousin Rollo will be imprisoned for affray. Two motifs coincide here: that of the impersonation by a 'double' of contrasted character and that of the girl who enters a marriage of convenience in order to rescue a male relation. Both are significant: the 'double' motif allows the author to explore different aspects of the female image, while the other provides a demonstration of the subordination of female interests to masculine ones.

In books which use this sacrifice motif – Heyer's *The Convenient Marriage* is a typical example – the heroine is placed in the position of sacrifice for a brother or other close male relative, who has brought the family into danger of bankruptcy and disrepute through his extravagance and irresponsibility – often through gambling. Both the element of sacrifice, with all its implicit injustice, and the use of the girl as a commodity – she is being sold to pay for her brother's debts, and her value is not so much in herself as in her cipher-like representation of an ancient and noble family – make the motif an emblem of all that the romances reject on women's behalf.

Though this situation is frequently found in a modified form, its implications are usually the same. Rollo, in *Bewitching Imposter*, is Shauna's cousin, but their relationship is very much that of brother and sister, and, although his irresponsibility is not gambling but getting drunk and fighting, the danger of disrepute is even more threatening, since he is likely to be put in a Tussharian gaol for his offence. And although the marriage of convenience was arranged for Ilena, not Shauna, the substitution of one for the other emphasizes its arbitrary nature; Shauna does not even know Alexis, far less want to marry him, and what the Tussharians are buying is not Shauna herself but a superficial likeness to Ilena.

The situation is presented as notably unfair to Shauna, and a cause of fear and suffering; even more than in other novels which use the motif, the book makes a protest against the use of a woman as either sacrifice or commodity – although in a 'safe' context, since the situation is so *outré* that it poses no real threat.

Shauna is Ilena's exact double, and the deception is not discovered. All the same, Alexis feels his bride has changed. Where Ilena is 'rigidly upright' – constrained by the artificial rules of society – Shauna has grown up 'free of fashion's constrictions'. Ilena is 'self-contained' (*and* corsetted: it is the difficulty of fitting her usual corset which reveals her condition); her thoughts 'are tutored to remain hidden', whereas Shauna's eyes, 'animated, reflected each passing thought' (p.85).

She is, in fact, the epitome of that natural innocence which so fascinates romantic writers; all the semes describing the two girls suggest that in each similar body is a unique essence, a true 'self', which their bodies will express unless they learn through the comportment imposed by society to hide and control it. Shauna represents an excess of nature, if such a thing is possible in romance: she comes to feel that she was wrong when, in her aunt's London house, she 'responded so innocently and spontaneously to the young exquisites' whom she met there by her talk of pig-catching and the like. The insight comes from her experience in being mastered by Alexis's masculine sexuality; for a woman to *express* innocence puts it in danger.

Ilena, on the other hand, has been over-socialized; in marrying Alexis she has taken on the sort of life later lived by her double - a round of empty ceremonial. Her selfhood will disappear, dispersed in the ritual of society. Ilena believes that she needs love to maintain her sense of identity; love is equated with experience in her mind: her mother, who presumably lived just such a life as she is anticipating for herself, is seen by her daughter as deprived, since she could never 'reach' her husband's heart. Ilena is determined 'not to go to *my* grave without knowing what true love could be'. If 'true love' brings ruin through her pregnancy, it brings fulfilment as a woman: 'I cannot regret my baby', she says. It fits the semi-parodic nature of the book that she is only too amply fulfilled by the birth of her twins.

Meanwhile, Shauna has begun to learn to curb nature and abide by the rules. Her innocent expressiveness, already seen as laying her open to redefinition by the 'exquisites' of London as sexual prey, both draws the hero to her and makes her vulnerable to his aggression. What attracts Alexis in Shauna is a combination of her innocence and natural expressiveness, something he is aware of lacking in himself. There is, however, an ambiguity in his feelings about her innocence which is especially evident in the description of the early part of their marriage: something in Alexis, hard and masculine as he is, responds to Shauna's ideal feminine qualities. He is unambiguously approving of Shauna's response to his kiss in the coach which bears them to their honeymoon in Hanaria; it 'set her limbs aquiver' but to him she gives 'the quivering lips of innocence' – and this excites him as well as making him feel protective (p.106). It is a reaction not unlike that of a number of romantic heroes. Tania Modleski has pointed out the importance of the romantic heroine's typical mixture of innocence and ability to arouse erotic feeling in allowing her to 'catch' a 'rich, lordly man' without appearing to be scheming – an ability to gain her ends only through passivity which emphasizes the heroine's subordinate role.[34] The hero's reaction is like that of those males in Gothic romances whose violence towards the heroine leads Joanna Russ to describe the books as 'a kind of justified paranoia'.[35] The motif expresses the danger of uncontrolled masculine violence; at the same time, it suggests Shauna's vulnerability and need for protection as Henrietta's need for protection was conveyed by Weyman in *Starvecrow Farm*.

Shauna's story develops both these aspects well beyond the normal limitations of female-centred romance. The image of masculinity as harsh and aggressive, threatening destruction to the fragile individuality of the woman within marriage, as it threatened use of her as sexual prey without, is here made startlingly plain, both through the events of the story and through the language and imagery.

As Shauna's marriage develops and changes, its locations change, the descriptions pointing up parallels between the places and the course of the marriage. Shauna has come from the natural marshes of her Irish childhood to the stiff artificiality of London; but she has always had dreams of a happy marriage to a man she loves. An illusory quality in marriage, however, is suggested by its taking place in Tusshar, so beautiful on the surface – a 'fairy-tale palace' – but also 'a place of deception and lies' (p.124). (It is also, of course, the home of the deceitful Ilena.)

On the wedding journey to her husband's Principality, they stop for a picnic in a pleasant dell, whose natural surroundings are the context for a brief idyllic interlude. Shauna is pleased to find her assertive, frightening husband has so pleasant a side to him, and he tells her that this had been a favourite spot during his childhood, which he had made 'his domain'. For him, clearly, the place reflects something essential about his nature, just as Shauna's marshlands did about Shauna, and the suggestion is that his aggressive masculinity is as false a mask as Ilena's corsetted self-control had been.

Yet as soon as they reach Hanaria, the Prince's country, she hears him 'shouting along the corridor in a hectoring voice after some unfortunate underling' (p.134). Hanarians have a reputation for harshness; aware of it, Alexis takes off his Hanarian medallion before he takes his Princess in his arms so that he comes to her 'no longer a Hanarian' (p. 115). The castle where the couple are to make their home is described in harsh, almost phallic terms: a 'stark fortress', 'bleak within . . . threatening without, dominating . . .' (p.230). If 'Tusshar' reflects Ilena, herself a symbol of over-socialized femininity, 'Hanaria' has the brutal qualities of unredeemed masculinity.

The description points up the threat which the relationship brings with it – of the masculinity which now dominates the vulnerable heroine. Most sinister of all, when Alexis embraces Shauna for the first time in the wedding carriage, her bouquet is crushed, and 'a blood-red petal lay on her skirt. For some inexplicable reason the sight disturbed her' (p.106). She is to suffer a fairly violent deflowering herself, not very different from rape.

The rhapsodic descriptions of kisses often hide or soften a pattern of dominance and submission characteristic of much of the love-making in these romances. Alexis 'throws Shauna forcefully on the bed' and pins her arms behind her back; when she struggles, 'the more his senses were inflamed'. Shauna's 'little devil of independence' is destroyed and she is 'powerless' in his hands. This expression of Alexis's raw masculine power is what presumably is seen to lie behind the illusions of the 'fairy-tale' dream of marriage. Yet at the same time Shauna feels the arousal of sexual responses: that very powerlessness springs not only from his brutality but from the 'wild delight' she feels in his love-making (pp.116, 117). Meanwhile, the 'magic' which her glances, expressive of her personality, have suggested begins in its turn to control *him*, so that more and more while he is with her the Alexis of the favourite dell comes to the surface. In this book it does not seem so much a matter of masculine transformation, as Radway has suggested,[36] as the liberation of a feminine side to the male which has been a part of him all

the time, as de Berault in Weyman's *Under the Red Robe* learned to
feel a part of the Cocheforêt's feminine world. In a way, the 'magic'
of women which controls men through, it seems, women's actual
vulnerability, suggests that there is a kind of power which women
can enjoy over men, so that the 'phallic castration' motif is there
despite the heroine's apparent weakness.

In *Bewitching Imposter*, it is some time before Shauna can come
into the full enjoyment of her power, since servants' gossip leads
Alexis into discovering the truth of the deception, and he turns
Shauna away in a fury. For a time she resumes her life as a débutante
in London. When, like Ilena, she discovers she is pregnant, however, she has to retire to her uncle's country house. Here Alexis
rediscovers her, looking after their child, and her tenderness towards it is enough to reawaken his feeling for her. He takes her back,
presumably to a happy marriage, though not to be a Princess: he is
able to act on his own account because in some Bonapartean
reshuffle of territory he has lost his Principality. In losing Hanaria
he is, of course, free to express the *un*-Hanarian feminine side of
himself. Like earlier heroes he retires to the feminine domain of
private life where the woman rules, even though in chains. Shauna's
personality has been threatened and even, in a sense, destroyed, but
she has been recreated as wife and mother and, the suggestion is,
this will compensate for the loss of the 'natural' Shauna.

In *Bewitching Imposter* love may thus seem a threat, but its link
with individual self-fulfilment, together with its 'magical' qualities
and role in solving female dilemmas in a patriarchal society, gives it
its own attractions. It is a reward which seems actually a part of the
way in which society is organized. If society is unfair to women, it is
an unfairness which brings its own rich rewards. In addition, it is
allied to qualities such as magnanimity and irreverence which are
portrayed as very positive values in society, counterbalancing its
competitive, over-individualistic nature.

This can help women readers to see contemporary society, with
all its faults, as the only structure in which true self-fulfilment can be
found, and so it validates the distribution of power between the
sexes in what is basically a patriarchal organization. Because of this,
women's romances, for all their air of protest, help to reinforce the
structures of society. Ann Rosalind Jones has described this process
of reinforcement after protest as a Barthesian 'inoculation effect':
an admission that an institution is liable to criticism which in itself

reinforces the status quo. 'The defence is phrased as "yes, but" . . . "yes, heterosexual courtship involves some inequities, but . . .".'[37]

Yet for Jones there remains an implicit protest in the romances which can be seen in the strains and contradictions of the narrative and discourse – such as the artificial quality of the erotic element in some of the narratives. Jones's example – a heroine who, in the middle of a cocktail party, 'aches to bear' the hero's children[38] – can be paralleled by the rather absurd use of phallic imagery in *Bewitching Imposter*: when the hero casts Shauna off she watches him as he 'absently began to stroke the jewelled handle of a small dagger' and at the sight 'her body ached for his touch' (p. 176) – the jewels symbolizing the value of the phallus for the heroine, presumably.

The contemporary romance combines both protest and reconciliation, but it does it in a familiar way. There *are* differences between *Bewitching Imposter* and the earlier romances described in this chapter. The Cinderella quality of Shauna's position (she is a poor relation of the ambassador), as well as the stress on the lack of sophistication in her surroundings, means that there is no suggestion in this book that a masculine attack on a lower-class girl might have been preferable to an affront to Shauna, as a lady. Male caring qualities are not associated with gentlemanliness and chivalry in *Bewitching Imposter*, as they are in other books, either. In fact, a cluster of associated concepts – aristocracy versus lower class, the nature of a gentleman, the connection of gentlemanly qualities with national feeling and a particular kind of government – seem to have vanished almost totally in this book, although there is a residue in the way Napoleon is presented as destroying the little individualistic Principalities which Britain is protecting. This is a genuine echo of the way in which England was presented in, say, *The White Company*, but is only a very minor element in the story. It may be that it is more difficult to express overt class attitudes in a romance written today; where class is mentioned it is often to protest against the arrogance of the upper classes, as in Sheila Bishop's *The Phantom Garden* (1974).

It is impossible to imagine Georgette Heyer writing a scene of virtual rape, as in *Bewitching Imposter*. Changes in attitudes towards sex, and a redrawing of the boundaries of what is acceptable in literature, after 1960 and the *Lady Chatterley* trial, have had some effect, evidently. *Bewitching Imposter* is not really typical of British romance, however; other romances are less explicit, although there is a good deal more physicality about the relationships described in books by writers like Mira Stables or Caroline Courtney than Heyer would ever have countenanced.

The continuities are more striking, however. 'The past' remains a site for traditional values – perhaps because this gives reassurance in a time of change, or perhaps because little essential has changed: in Jones's words, change is unlikely given continuing 'economic, social and psychic forces'.[39] So in the historical romance of the present day, as in the past, it is important to show the woman's world of tenderness and personal relationships as being at the same time important and fragile, so that the traditional relationship between the sexes is by implication necessary for the continuance of a civilized society.

Chapter 8

History, best-sellers and the media

In the hands of Georgette Heyer historical romances ceased to be primarily stories of adventure and became love stories with an appeal to a mainly female audience. Heyer changed the function of the genre without radically changing the form. This is only one of the ways in which the genre has been adapted to new functions throughout the course of its history. In the period between 1890 and 1900, for instance, these adaptations echoed attitudes among the readers which arose from the dwindling of Britain's status in the world and from changes in society. Like those of other popular genres[1] the texts normalize such attitudes and make any contradictions they may reveal less evident, although they also allow the expression of protest to some extent.

This is only one example of the ways in which such texts function. The discussion of themes and attitudes in the preceding chapters show that historical romances in general used their historical backgrounds to address important contemporary issues, some of which remained important throughout the period, while others were more specific to a particular phase of the genre. The development of the genre between 1890 and 1990 falls into four broad phases. In the first, which runs roughly from 1890 to the outbreak of the First World War, authors such as Conan Doyle, Weyman and Mason wrote adventure stories whose historical settings made some pretension to be an accurate picture of the past. The periods they favoured were ones of historical change, when new phases of economic and social development could be portrayed as embryonic forms of contemporary institutions, progressing through a natural and beneficent process of social evolution. Such portrayals could help to smooth over points of strain and dysfunction within contemporary society; at a time when organized labour was challenging traditional power relationships in a series of strikes, and suffragette agitation was increasing, Weyman's pictures of the development of a ruling class who saw their function as a form of service must have been reassuring.

By the time of the First World War signs of change were already evident in the genre. Although the books Rafael Sabatini and Baroness Orczy wrote during the 1900s had much in common with those of their older contemporaries – detailed historical settings, for example, and a preference for periods of change – the element of outdoor adventure was less important, and the focus was upon charismatic heroes and glamorous settings. In 1910 Jeffery Farnol's *The Broad Highway* made little pretence of providing historical accuracy: a little blood, some love amongst the aristocracy, and a nostalgic picture of an idyllic pre-industrial English countryside were the ingredients which made this book a best-seller.

After the First World War it was this kind of swashbuckling, glamorous novel which was dominant, providing a sense of escape into a more colourful world for men and women still traumatized by the experience of war and living in a difficult post-war world. This may have been the chief function of the romances in this second phase, which covers the years immediately before and after the First World War; it is interesting that the preferred settings were the late eighteenth and early nineteenth centuries, that is, just before England finally lost its essentially rural character. The stories were personal, rather than political, as though the task of presenting a reassuring picture of contemporary social and political life was now an impossible one; even heroes who engage in public activity, like Rafael Sabatini's Scaramouche, escape from it in horror at the consequences of their actions at the end of the novel.

Georgette Heyer's novels introduced a new phase which, beginning in the mid-1920s, ran for some time concurrently with the swashbucklers – which continued to be written during the lifetime of their authors, so that the second phase only really died away in the 1940s. Heyer's books appealed to female readers for whom issues concerned with the role of women in a time of rapid change were becoming increasingly important. Although the unfairness of the treatment of women was more evident in the post-war world, after women had been showing themselves capable of moving out of their traditional roles into the wider world of men's work, this could appear as threatening; the situations of the texts exposed the injustices and the fears arising from female vulnerability and proposed a reassuring solution in terms of traditional marriage. Such concerns are less tied to a particular time than the fears of war and war-weariness which made the swashbucklers appealing; fears of women moving out of traditional roles were also a feature of the early years of the century when suffragette agitation was at its height, and when Weyman addressed them in *Starvecrow Farm* in 1904 he used situations which evoked similar attitudes.

The Heyer phase has lasted to the present day, and historical romance continues to be a genre which appeals to women; but in the 1970s and 1980s other issues, such as praise for the hardworking and deserving rich, have become more important, forming a fourth phase. The romances represent, perhaps, a validation of attitudes which might be held with some feeling of discomfort since they fly in the face of traditional moral ideas such as the importance of care for the weak or service to the community. They are none the less attitudes which have actually existed, certainly in the 1980s.

If the romances fulfil varying functions at various times, it is through slight differences of presentation and focus rather than through radical changes in the nature of the stories or the characters, which have remained essentially the same throughout the twentieth century. The same patterns of relationship between hero and heroine, and the same plot motifs, can be seen in both the outdoor adventure stories of Weyman or Conan Doyle in the 1890s and in the social comedies of Heyer in the 1920s or of her followers in the 1980s. Moreover, the changing functions have one general function in common: that of normalizing traditional attitudes and patterns of behaviour when rapid changes in society seemed to threaten the status quo.

In helping texts to fulfil this normalizing function,the historical element is useful because it appears to provide a 'background' of neutral fact to an imaginary story – whereas in fact it is an imaginative creation itself, infused with authorial ideology. Although it is possible to find examples of popular texts which try to expose rather than affirm existing power relationships, there are features of this particular genre which make such exposure difficult.

These points may be illustrated by a brief comparison between the dominant attitudes which have been noted in historical romance, and the ways in which they have been symbolized in the texts, with those in other kinds of popular historical text. First, though, an examination of the changes in function of some of the

generic motifs which have survived in historical romance throughout the period from 1890 to 1990 will give some idea of the ways in
which changing contemporary attitudes can be reflected in the texts
of a relatively unchanging genre.

One such motif – although it is one which, as it happens, is not
confined to historical romance – is the wounding or sickness of the
hero, usually combined with the heroine's tending of him. Tony
Bennett and Janet Woollacott[2] have pointed out the frequency of
this motif in romances, whether historical or not, arguing that it
represents a diminution of the hero's phallic power which helps to
equalize the relationship between hero and heroine as a basis for a
marriage which is essentially a partnership.

There is certainly a good deal of evidence in both male-centred
and female-centred texts that the motif will bear this interpretation.
That it can be seen as empowering the heroine – too much, perhaps,
for the reader's taste – is suggested by the number of occasions on
which the heroine's actions on behalf of the hero are immediately
followed by a display of some kind of feminine weakness – fainting
into the hero's arms, for instance.[3] In the earlier, male-centred,
romances, however, a more dominant impression is that the heroine
is developing from a girl, full of whims and fancies, into a woman
who is ready to fulfil a 'truly feminine' role. Power – of a kind – is an
important part of such a role, but it is a power of maintaining, not of
initiating: of feeling, not of doing. The girl becomes, in fact, not only
a wife-to-be, but a woman capable of motherhood. It is a transition
which is symbolized more than once in Weyman's work of the 1890s
and 1900s by a particular form of the 'heroine tending the hero'
motif: the return of the hero's son (from a previous marriage) as a
gift of the heroine to the hero.[4]

In the 'female-centred' romance of Heyer and her followers,
from the mid-1920s onwards, the meaning of the 'wounded hero'
motif has changed to some extent, to become much closer to that
suggested by Bennett and Woollacott. Its use in Georgette Heyer's
Devil's Cub (1932) is a case in point. The heroine of this novel, Mary
Challoner, is not a child on the verge of womanhood; though still
young, she is mature in her attitudes and capable of the kind of self-
sacrifice which in earlier heroines had first been called for by the
hero's need. In fact, the plot is set in motion by her risking the ruin
of her own reputation in order to save her flighty sister from being
seduced and then (Mary fears) abandoned by the Marquis of Vidal.
The result is that the angry Vidal tries to rape her and she shoots

him. Having shot him, she is overcome with remorse – proper female tenderness is still much in evidence in Heyer's work – and stays by him to look after him until his wound heals. There can be no doubt that this gives her a kind of dominance over Vidal; she bullies him into eating gruel and orders him not to leave his bed. This has a degree of equalizing power which outlasts Vidal's illness, since he now takes her seriously as a girl to marry, not to seduce; but 'normal' male dominance is resumed when Vidal, recovered, insists on becoming Mary's protector. One kind of dominance – the use of a weapon, with its phallic suggestions – is thus by implication rejected (through Mary's remorse), and a more feminine kind, which does not threaten the established pattern, displaces it.

In the 'female-centred' romances the heroine's tenderness is thus still an important element of the motif: in *Devil's Cub* Mary is not so much giving promise of eventual motherliness, as acting as though she *were* Vidal's mother. The motif here, however, is part of the construction of a heroine who is much more independent than those of Weyman or Orczy. Later in the novel, Mary is shown chafing against the restrictions enforced by the suddenly strict and patriarchal Vidal, in much the same way as other heroines – like Judith in *Regency Buck* – resent the limitations imposed by society on the 'pure' female in order to protect not her but her chastity. The motif takes its place in the picture of a society which is unfair to women, even if it gives them a compensation in the love of a powerful male, rather than adding to the 'angel in the house' image, which was its function in the male-centred romances.

Bennett and Woollacott suggest that the diminution of male power which the motif entails in the work of Heyer and her followers is part of the pleasure of the romantic text for a female reader,[5] and it may be that it is because it contains such motifs that the historical romance continued as a female literary form long after it had ceased to be of compelling interest to men.

There are some themes which remain the same throughout the century, suggesting stable attitudes which continue despite some surface changes. One of these is the portrayal of class. In the texts there are two classes normally portrayed, neither of them the middle class to which many of the readers probably belonged. Where middle-class characters are portrayed, it is usually as *nouveau riche* intruders into the aristocracy, but it is the aristocratic hero or heroine with whom the reader is invited to identify. In the earlier, male-centred romances written at the turn of the nineteenth century, this meant that the upper classes could be portrayed as natural rulers, although the fact that such heroes are drawn from the minor aristocracy, who are given what power they have by a patron, rather than from the great magnates means that they could be used to represent a professionalism not unlike that of public servants in the late nineteenth or early twentieth century. The heroes thus took their place as part of the presentation of a 'good' state which could be seen as a forerunner to the liberal state at the turn of the century, and helped to validate it.

In later, female-centred romances from the inter-war and post-Second World War period, when to promote such an idea of the state was of less importance – partly because of a more general acceptance of corporatism in the years after the First World War, and partly because of the foregrounding of concerns more relevant to a female readership, such as relationships between the sexes – the hero is drawn from a higher class – that of the great hereditary landowners – which gives him more charisma and power.

In both masculine and feminine romance, however, the treatment of class is the same: upper-class characters are seen as belonging to what amounts to a different species from lower-class ones, as the Abbot of Beaulieu is physically more refined than the animal-like John of Hordle in Conan Doyle's *The White Company* (1891), or as Clare Darcy's Letty can be recognized as aristocratic despite her lower-class diguise by the refinement of her features (*Letty*, 1980). This is not an attitude confined to historical romances but its significance in the presentation of 'history' is that it confirms the idea of the upper classes as natural rulers.

This attitude colours the presentation of such favourite generic motifs as that of rebellion: the rebellions in both Weyman's *The Abbess of Vlaye* (1904) and Barbara Cartland's *The Proud Princess* (1976) are presented sympathetically because they are supported by aristocrats and enable *good* members of the upper class (disinterested, with an ideal of service and a respect for freedom) to take the place of tyrannical rulers. Rebellions which are purely of the people, like the uprising of the Jacquerie against Sir Tristram de Villefranche, may be presented as inevitable because of the tyranny of the nobles but there is little sympathy with the actual rebellion, which is portrayed as a horrific event.

The ideological 'messages' of the texts, whether modified during the course of the century, or remaining constant throughout the sequence of romances, have in common a relationship to the issues that were important at the time in which the books were written. The image of 'Englishness' illustrates this. It was an important image in the romances of the 1890s and 1900s. At a time when Britain was beginning to lose her economic predominance, a sense of English superiority could be confirmed by the presentation of 'English' qualities in the romances of Weyman, Conan Doyle, Sabatini or Orczy. If the Englishmen of the past were as chivalric, independent, sensible and freedom-loving as they were portrayed by these writers, such qualities, on which English supremacy was based, were clearly no accident of economic history but inherent in all the English. Moreover, the English were connected as though by an umbilical cord with the land of England itself, presented as essentially rural: a green countryside studded with homogeneous communities where men might work together with satisfaction and a sense of pride in their craft. Such a country was worth fighting for in time of war.

These images may seem irrelevant to female-centred romance, since 'Englishness' was presented as an essentially masculine quality, inherent in masculine institutions (see p.67). None the less, presumably women do not want to feel they live in a second- or third-class country any more than men do, and English female-centred romances from the 1900s to the present show traces of the 'English' image too: the hero of Heyer's *Powder and Patch* (1923) may seem foppishly Frenchified, but underneath his silks and make-up beats a steadfast English heart; and Harry, the hero of Clare Darcy's *Letty*, may seem a cosmopolitan, but he is sufficiently awake to the dangers of Letty's planned marriage to a foreign nobleman with a foreigner's lack of true respect for the purity of womanhood to drag her away from the altar and so save her reputation.

Elements of the 'English' concept are also used in female-centred romances to express attitudes towards specifically female issues. English qualities develop best in a state of freedom and proximity to nature. Examples may be found in the male-centred adventure romances as well as in the 'female' ones. Rafael Sabatini's *The Hounds of God* (1928) was written at a time when Heyer's historical romances for women were already becoming best-sellers. Sabatini is essentially a writer whose books belong to the second phase of twentieth-century historical romance, centred round charismatic heroes; but this novel, perhaps in response to Heyer's popularity, allows the heroine an important role. Margaret Trevannion is allowed by her father an unusual freedom as a girl to wander the moors of her native Devon, and grows up refreshingly open, honest and rational – qualities in strong opposition to the deviousness and bigotry of her enemies, the Spaniards.

The naturalness of the heroine was to become an important attribute; it is significant in the work of Heyer and her followers in the third phase of historical romance because it surrounds the heroine with attractive associations, allowing the reader to sympathize with her fight against the petty regulations which limit the role of women. The limitations, in destroying something so valuable as the heroine's unfettered individuality, are made to seem all the more unfair.

Even though the 'messages' of historical romance therefore tend to confirm contemporary attitudes and power relationships, the genre can be used to express protest as well. On the other hand, the reading of romance can blunt the edge of protest because of the compensatory features of the resolution, features which form a large part of the pleasure of the text, such as the revelation that the hero's often unaccountable behaviour is due to his love for the heroine.[6] Within the text, too, the interpellatory devices which enable the reader to form an empathetic identification with one or other of the characters also make him or her assume, temporarily, the 'natural' social relationships and attitudes constructed by the cues in the text.[7] If the confirmatory aspect of historical romance ultimately dominates the subversive aspect it is because like other popular fiction it encourages a particular kind of reading: a role-play of the imagination which involves the reader so intimately in the text that the maintaining of any kind of critical distance becomes difficult.

The impression given of 'history' in these novels can be summed up as an imaginative creation, a selective version of the past which embodies concepts of a 'natural' hierarchical society. Its chief function is to confirm attitudes current at the time of writing, although the presentation allows a certain amount of protest and subversion of such attitudes – usually 'made safe' by the ending which appears to provide a resolution of any problems raised in the text.

The 'historical' and the romantic elements of the genre thus combine to provide a function common in popular fiction; what is specific to the genre is the way in which 'history' can be used to address specific kinds of issue, such as the nature of government or the national character. Historical romance has flourished most when such issues were most under debate, as at the turn of the century, when in the hands of Stanley Weyman and his imitators it was the predominant genre.[8]

It became a dominant genre again in the mid-1920s – although as a sub-genre of women's romance in general – because 'history' also provided a useful means by which issues concerned with the role and nature of women could be raised: a past society can be shaped into a fantasy world with features extrapolated from those in the reader's own society which have a bearing on such issues, without losing the sense of reality. The most obvious example is that of Heyer's picture of Regency society; one in which the actions of unmarried women were highly regulated and constrained, while men were tacitly allowed a good deal of self-indulgence, a situation which accentuated inequalities in male and female roles. That it was also an exaggeration, rather than a true picture, can be seen by looking at biographies and other documents of the life of the period: Lady Caroline Lamb, for instance, had a good deal more freedom of action than Heyer's romances suggest was possible for women.[9]

In addressing different issues the genre necessarily changed to some extent – foregrounding love instead of adventure, for instance, or social history rather than political events, although this was a change in proportion rather than an elimination of any of the elements traditional in the genre. Within the past two decades historical fiction has been subject to similar changes to address the needs of a new generation. In 1987 a librarian noted that romances of the traditional pattern were by then largely the choice of older women, looking for the kind of reading material to which they were used – although Mills & Boon still produce 'traditional' historical romances as part of their output, so the market for such books still remains to some extent.

Sagas, with their links with the domestic novel and their use of the more recent past, now predominate on the shelves of book-sellers and on the best-seller lists.[10] The setting – often the end of the nineteenth and the early twentieth century[11] – can be presented as a period suited to individual initiative, making possible the rapid rise in the family fortunes which are a feature of this genre. At the time when such stories were gaining in popularity – the late 1970s and 1980s – this may have suited the contemporary mood better: the 1980s were, after all, the period of the 'Yuppie', when it seemed possible for a time that vast wealth could be gained quickly.

In some ways, too, the sagas allowed the construction of a new image of femininity, one more in tune with a period of greater opportunity for women, when 'liberation' was a much canvassed issue: the business-woman heroine, who constructs a retail empire with her own efforts after a struggle with hardship which has toughened her, was a more 'modern' image for the late 1970s and 1980s. It had affinities with 'power-dressing' and with the 'villainess' of soap-opera – a similarly tough figure – which, Tania Modleski has suggested, allows 'the spectator . . . to watch the villainess as she tries to gain control over her feminine passivity, thereby acting out the spectator's fantasies of power'.[12]

The effect of such changes on the image of women must not be exaggerated, of course. The identification of the reader or spectator with figures such as the tough heroine or the unscrupulous villainess is unlikely to be as complete as it was with earlier, more conventional heroines. This is because in some ways they represent an inversion of traditional female values which can be enjoyed as 'an outlet for feminine anger'[13] even while the reader or spectator is concurrently identifying with the forces which may frustrate the villainess's projects.[14] The business-woman heroine might provide a more suitable vehicle for female aspiration, but usually operates in a 'feminine' space within the business world – as a fashion designer, or as the head of a department store, the core of which is the fashion department - as Estella Tincknell has pointed out.[15]

What the sagas also offer is one feature which is present also in more traditional historical romance, but which is more strongly accentuated in the sagas, with their more recent setting, just beyond the bounds of memory for most readers: a nostalgia for an idealized world in which individual effort could be rewarded, but within a stable, hierarchical setting. In Barbara Taylor Bradford's *A Woman of Substance* (1980), for instance, the heroine's rise from the working class to a position of power and wealth seems more in tune with a modern idea of 'classlessness' than the images of class presented by historical romance, but she is shown as an unusual individual. She cuts herself off completely from her working-class roots, and when she revisits her old home her old associates are in general portrayed as inferior to her, and expected by her to 'know their place'.[16] A reassuring picture is painted, of a world in which 'classlessness' is possible but class differences remain nevertheless the same.

Historical fiction of any kind has always been well suited to validating ingrained attitudes by suggesting that they are 'natural' because sanctified by long tradition. Such a validation is reassuring: it fits the kind of nostalgia which Patrick Wright saw as an uneasiness with modernity in a time of rapid change and a desire for traditional values which need no questioning.[17] Historical fiction could do more than suggest the existence of a society in which such values were dominant: it could *reconstruct* one, putting flesh on the bones of the past in the way that Stephen Bann's taxidermist reconstructed the dead animals.[18] For a brief time a reader could have the experience of living in 'history'. Today, that experience is available through other media, which depend less on the active use of the imagination and give a greater sense of immediate reality.

Historical 'recreation' seems particularly popular just now, perhaps because of a continuing sense of a problematic present, perhaps because we now have the technology to creat more 'accurate' images of the past – a sense of 'how it was', apparently without glamorization, like the Viking exhibition in York with its synthetic but 'authentic' smells. There is clearly a felt need for such recreations, as though to experience the past, warts and all, allows us to live more comfortably in the present – perhaps by suggesting that behind all the differences there lies an essential continuity.

For all such television programmes, theme parks and exhibitions use 'recreation' to give an authentication to an ideologically charged image of the past – like the 1940s street and living room in 'Eden Camp', the ex-prisoner-of-war camp turned Second World War exhibition near Malton in Yorkshire. This exhibition provides charts and information which, in limited space, attempt to give a balanced picture of the era, and the general presentation includes a clear impression of its horrors. Some of the reconstructions, however, have an undoubtedly nostalgic atmosphere which carries its own ideological charge. One portrays a 'typical' living room, with a model family sitting close to the radio listening to news of the war. The implication is that behind all the temporary 'horrors' in the world of historical events, symbolized by the taped 'news' emanating from the radio, lies a 'normal' English life based on a family life consisting of mother, father and child gathered together in a kind of equality; this reconstruction comes after a German scene, not of a household but of a beer cellar. The living-room image suggests a nation of small individual families linked to the 'central' policy-making element of the nation by its organ, the 'classless' radio with its 'neutral' newsreader. It is reinforced by a later reconstruction of a street in which a shop window shows household goods (suggesting old-fashioned home-making when housewives took a pride in keeping the house clean with no hankering after careers outside) mingled with the apparatus of children's seasonal games – whips, tops and skipping ropes – reminiscent of a stable world of traditional and innocent pastimes, far from the fashion-orientated 'youth culture' of the 1990s.

Such nostalgia and reassurance is so much part of the pleasure of recreations of the past that it is difficult to see how popular presentations of history can avoid them altogether. Some have tried, however, to minimize the element of reassurance and to give a popular image of society in the past which lays bare the nature of some of the power relationships which were taken for granted and abuses of power which accompanied them.

One example was the television series *A Secret World of Sex* shown on BB2 in April and May 1991. The programmes used traditionally 'nostalgic' settings: holidays in Blackpool between the wars, for example; or the 'Upstairs, Downstairs' world of the middle-class household with servants from the end of the last century to the end of the Second World War. There was little nostalgia about the presentation, however; the experiences described were uncomfortable ones, suggestive of a world in which sexuality was furtive, almost criminalized. It included the testimony of women who had been incarcerated in mental hospitals for years because of under-age sexual activity – once considered a sign of mental disease – or who, as servants, had lost their jobs ignominiously because they had been sexually abused by their masters. That the effects of such abuse persist into the present was made plain, since the still-felt bitterness of the witnesses for wasted opportunities and wasted lives was clear. For one viewer at least the programme had a potent effect in countering nostalgia: a Brighton viewer wrote to the *Radio Times* to say that

> After watching *A Secret World of Sex: Acts of Violence* (21 May BBC2) I wept with sorrow and anger at the tragedy of the poor lady who had spent 70 years in a mental hospital because she was a rape victim all those years ago . . . Those who harp on about 'the good old days' should watch this programme.[19]

Series such as these deal with the same issues as historical romance does, but the effect is very different, making any kind of complacent reading difficult.

On the other hand, it would be a mistake to suppose that all reading of historical romance *is* complacent and uncritical. One effect of viewing popular fiction as a kind of imaginative holiday, as suggested by Pierre Bourdieu,[20] is that some readers, at least, draw a line in their minds between the attitudes of a popular text and 'reality', which enables them to identify ideological messages which conflict with their experience and aspirations and disregard them even while momentarily assuming them. One reader, for example, who enjoys reading Georgette Heyer's books, feels that she 'got really involved with the characters' while at the same time feeling that the books were 'exasperating' because they were 'sexist' and the outcome – the heroine melting into the hero's arms – was always the same.[21] The pleasure which came from a Heyer text was, for this reader, not unlike that of an avowed fantasy text such as the stories of David Eddings. These, in turn, can be connected with other images which give a fantasy of exaggerated masculinity: those of heavy metal rock bands, for example. Historical romance, fantasy text and cult music seem to inhabit a similar world of the imagination, enjoyed with a sense that the act of doing so is a kind of game, not to be taken too seriously. Implicit in this game is the acceptance of attitudes which would not normally be approved at all.

Such evidence suggests that the messages individual readers take from popular texts are as various as their cultural contexts. This is something which must be borne in mind when considering the 'meaning' of any text. Historical romance does address particular issues relevant to the period in which it is written; and the cues which prompt a reading in line with contemporary attitudes can be discovered in the texts. For many readers, particularly those reading the books when they were first published, the meanings prompted by such cues were probably dominant. But this does not mean that cues for other readings – ones which contradict or subvert dominant attitudes – cannot be found in the texts, perhaps despite the intentions of the author. If some readers are aware of the nature of the genre – that is, if they can read the books with a sense of amusement or even exasperation at the ideological messages, even while giving themselves up to the story – this suggests that the atttitudes of the books are not simply accepted uncritically, and that the 'disappearing act' which Tania Modleski has suggested is typical of the reading of romance[22], by which the reader loses a sense of her own individuality, is neither universal nor necessarily complete. So that, finally, if the 'mythical' quality of a historical setting carries a potent ideological charge, which it clearly does, the ideological element may not always be received uncritically at every reading.

Notes

1 Introduction

1 G. Beer, *Romance*, London, 1970, p. 2.
2 ibid.
3 M. Williamson, 'The Greek Romance', in J. Radford (ed.), *The Progress of Romance*, London, 1986, p. 32.
4 J. A. Hodge, *The Private World of Georgette Heyer*, London, 1984, p. 7.
5 U. Eco, 'Reflections on *The Name of the Rose*', *Encounter*, LXIV, 4 April 1985, p. 17.
6 U. Eco, *Travels in Hyper-reality*, tr. W. Weaver, London, 1987, p. 69.
7 ibid., p. 68.
8 ibid.
9 J. Radway, *Reading the Romance: Women, Patriarchy and Popular Literature*, Chapel Hill, 1984, pp. 196–7.
10 H. Henderson, *Versions of the Past*, New York, 1974, p. 13.
11 R. Chapman, *The Victorian Debate*, London, 1968, p. 13.
12 A. Fleishman, *The English Historical Novel: Walter Scott to Virginia Woolf*, Baltimore, 1971, p. 17.
13 S. Bann, *The Clothing of Clio*, Cambridge, 1984, p. 6.
14 Beer, op. cit., p. 65.
15 ibid.
16 Henderson, op. cit., p. 8.
17 C. Cockburn, *Bestseller*, London, 1972, p. 103.
18 Bann, op. cit., p. 5.
19 R. Barthes, *Mythologies*, tr. A. Lavers, London, 1973, p. 142.
20 Cockburn, op. cit., p. 98.
21 G. Avery, 'The Very Pink of Propriety', *The Times Literary Supplement* (21 September 1984), p. 1064.
22 G. Martin, '*Readers, Viewers and Texts*', Unit 13, in *Popular Culture*, Open University Course U203, Milton Keynes, 1981, p. 24.

2 The structures of historical romance

1 R. Barthes, *Mythologies*, tr. A. Lavers, London, 1973, p. 142.

2 R. Brunt, 'A Career in Love: The Romantic World of Barbara Cart-land', in C. Pawling (ed.), *Popular Fiction and Social Change*, London, 1984, p. 145.
3 Vladimir Propp, in *The Morphology of the Folktale* (Austin, Texas, 1968, originally published in Russian in 1928), isolated seven character functions in folk tale: villain, helper, donor, sought-for person and her father, dispatcher, hero, false hero.
4 According to Jane Aiken Hodge's biography of Georgette Heyer, *The Private World of Georgette Heyer* (London, 1984, p. 25), it was the publication of this romance which attracted a new and largely female audience to Heyer's work.
5 R. Barthes, 'The Reality Effect', in Tz. Todorov (ed.), *French Literary Theory Today*, tr. R. Carter, Cambridge, 1982, p. 16.
6 C. Dickens, *A Tale of Two Cities*, ed. G. Woodcock, Harmondsworth, 1985 (first published 1859), p. 59.
7 J. Radway, *Reading the Romance: Women, Patriarchy and Popular Literature*, Chapel Hill, 1984, p. 107.
8 W. Scott, *Rob Roy*, London, 1963 (first published 1807), p. 7.
9 U. Eco, '*Casablanca:* Cult Movies and Inter-textual Collage', in *Travels in Hyper-Reality*, tr. W. Weaver, London, 1987, p. 200.
10 B. Tomashevski, quoted in R. Selden, *A Reader's Guide to Contemporary Literary Theory*, London, 1985, p. 13.
11 Eco, op cit.
12 D. Dean, *The Briar Rose*, London, 1986, p. 8.
13 Radway, op. cit., pp. 193–4.
14 The 'few herrings' are from a revolutionary 'fraternal supper' described in E. Orczy, *The Triumph of the Scarlet Pimpernel*, London, 1969 (first published 1922), p. 48. The floors of the Fisherman's Rest are described in E. Orczy, *The Scarlet Pimpernel*, London, 1961 (first published 1905), p. 126.
15 Brunt, op. cit., p. 146.
16 Dean, op. cit., p. 8.
17 P. Bourdieu, quoted in J. Donald and C. Mercer, 'Reading and Realism', in *Popular Culture*, Unit 15, Open University Course U203, Milton Keynes, 1981, p. 71.
18 R. Barthes, *S/Z*, tr. R. Miller, London, 1975, p. 18.
19 R. Barthes, 'The Reality Effect', p. 16.
20 W. Iser, *The Implied Reader*, Baltimore, 1974.
21 Barthes, 'The Reality Effect', p. 18.

3 The readers of historical romance

1 C. Cockburn, *Bestseller*, London, 1972, p. 3.
2 ibid.
3 F. Bédarida, *A Social History of England*, tr. A. S. Forster, London, 1979, p. 52.
4 ibid.
5 D. Altick, *The English Common Reader*, Chicago, 1967 (1957), p. 359.
6 ibid., p. 361.
7 ibid., pp. 311, 313.

8 ibid., p. 306.
9 R. Williams, *The Long Revolution*, Harmondsworth, 1980 (1961), p. 169.
10 Bédarida, op. cit., p. 52.
11 Williams, op. cit., p. 169.
12 D. Thomson, *England in the Nineteenth Century: 1815–1914*, Harmondsworth, 1959 (1950), p. 205.
13 ibid.
14 Q. D. Leavis, *Fiction and the Reading Public*, London, 1965 (first published 1932), pp. 26, 17 and 28.
15 R. Bromley, *Lost Narratives*, London, 1988, p. 136.
16 P. Wright, *On Living in an Old Country: The National Past in Contemporary Britain*, London, 1985.
17 ibid., p. 16.
18 D. Thomson, op. cit., p. 194.
19 A. Marwick, *Britain in the Century of Total War: War, Peace and Social Change, 1900–1967*, Harmondsworth, 1968, p. 10.
20 ibid.
21 ibid.
22 Bédarida, op. cit., p. 180.
23 M. Weiner, *English Culture and the Decline of the Industrial Spirit 1850–1980*, Cambridge, 1981.
24 E.g. Eric Hobsbaum, in *Industry and Empire* (Harmondsworth, 1968, p. 183), agrees that there is some truth in the 'gentrification' theory but feels that the decline in industrial growth can be put down to the early beginnings of industrialization in Britain.
25 Bédarida, op. cit., p. 288.
26 Thomson, op. cit., p. 203.
27 Marwick, op. cit., p. 19.
28 ibid., p. 141.
29 Bédarida, op. cit., p. 275.
30 S. Hall, C. Critcher, T. Jefferson, J. Clarke and B. Roberts, *Policing the Crisis*, Basingstoke, 1978, p. 147.
31 Bédarida, op. cit., p. 93.
32 W. Ashworth, *An Economic History of England, 1870–1939*, London, 1960, p. 241.
33 Marwick, op. cit., p. 21.
34 Bédarida, op. cit., p. 48.
35 ibid., p. 47.
36 Bédarida, op. cit., p. 52.
37 Bédarida, op. cit., p. 90.
38 ibid., p. 91.
39 Coventry Patmore, *Poems*, vol. 2, London, 1879.
40 Bédarida, op. cit., p. 188.
41 ibid., p. 92.
42 Thomson, op. cit., p. 188.
43 ibid.
44 ibid.
45 Bédarida, op. cit., p. 82.
46 Thomson, op. cit., pp. 201, 202.

47 D. Sutton, 'Liberalism, State Collectivism and the Social Relations of Citizenship', in M. Langan and Bill Schwarz (eds), *Crises in the British State, 1880–1930*, London, 1985, p. 72 (Spencer had published his analogy in 1850).
48 ibid.
49 R. Colls, 'Englishness and the National Culture', in R. Colls and P. Dodd (eds), *Englishness: Politics and Culture, 1880–1920*, London, 1986, p. 52.
50 ibid.
51 Bédarida, op. cit., p. 84.
52 Cockburn, op. cit., p. 95.
53 ibid., p. 103.
54 Marwick, op. cit., p. 48.
55 ibid., p. 47 for an account of the women's suffrage movement, and p. 41 for an account of the strikes.
56 Cockburn, op. cit., p. 103.
57 Rafael Sabatini's best-known books, *Scaramouche* and *Captain Blood* were published in 1921 and 1922 respectively. His last work was published in 1949.
58 Cockburn, op. cit., p. 95.
59 J. A. Hodge, *The Private World of Georgette Heyer*, London, 1984, p. 17.
60 ibid., p. 7.
61 A. R. Jones, 'Mills & Boon Meets feminism', in J. Radford (ed.), *The Progress of Romance*, London, 1986, p. 198.
62 J. Langham, press release on behalf of Mills & Boon, October 1986.
63 Hodge, op. cit., p. 7.
64 P. Mann, 'Romantic Fiction and its Readership', *Poetics* 14, nos. 1/2, April 1985, p. 2.
65 G. Heyer, *The Quiet Gentleman*, London, 1951, p. 1.
66 ibid.
67 J. Radway, *Reading the Romance, Women, Patriarchy and Popular Literature*, Chapel Hill, 1984; R. Brunt, 'A Career in Love: The Romantic World of Barbara Cartland' in C. Pawling (ed.), *Popular Fiction and Social Change*, London, 1984, p. 146.
68 D. Riley, 'The Free Mothers: Pro-natalism and Working Mothers in Industry at the End of the Last War in Britain, *History Workshop*, 11, Spring 1981, pp. 59–120.
69 D. Thomson, *England in the Twentieth Century*, Harmondsworth, 1965, p. 122.
70 A. Swingewood, *The Myth of Mass Culture*, London, 1977, p. x.

4 Evolution versus revolution

1 R. Colls, 'Englishness and the Political Culture' in R. Colls and P. Dodd (eds), *Englishness: Politics and Culture 1880–1920*, London, 1986.
2 M. Arnold, *Culture and Anarchy*, in *Selected Essays*, ed. N. Annan, London, 1964, p. 296.
3 M. Girouard, *The Return to Camelot*, New Haven, 1981, p. 62.
4 *Casino Royale* was published in 1955; *The White Company* in 1891.

5 T. Bennett and J. Woollacott, *Bond and Beyond: The Political Career of a Popular Hero*, London, 1987.
6 ibid., p. 104.
7 ibid., p. 105.
8 ibid., p. 104.
9 ibid., p. 105.
10 Marc Girouard, in *The Return to Camelot*, traces the construction of the ideal gentleman current in the Victorian and, to a lesser extent, in the Edwardian period to the impact of works like *The Broadstone of Honour* of 1832: the distinctive virtues of the chivalrous man were 'belief and trust in God, generosity, high honour, independence, truthfulness, loyalty to friends and leaders, hardihood and contempt of luxury, courtesy, modesty, humanity and respect for women' (Girouard, op. cit., p. 62). Sir Nigel is a good example of the chivalrous man of Digby's picture: he tells his squire that he is going to France to combat 'wrongs, tyrannies, infamies and wrongings of damsels' (A. Conan Doyle, *The White Company*, London, 1891, p. 158).
11 A. Conan Doyle, *Sir Nigel* (first published in 1906), in *The Conan Doyle Historical Romances*, vol. 1, London, 1931, p. 432.
12 G. Lukacs, *The Historical Novel*, tr. H. and S. Mitchell, London, 1962, p. 28.
13 R. Barthes, *Mythologies*, tr. A. Lavers, London, 1973, p. 116.
14 Arnold, op. cit., pp. 268–71.

5 English heritage

1 C. Cockburn, *Bestseller*, London, 1972, p. 103.
2 S. Hall *et al.*, *Policing the Crisis*, Basingstoke, 1978, p. 147.
3 ibid.
4 P. Dodd, 'Englishness and the National Culture', in R. Colls and P. Dodd (eds), *Englishness; Politics and Culture 1880–1920*, London, 1986, pp. 1–22.
5 ibid., p. 2.
6 ibid., p. 7.
7 E. Showalter, *A Literature of their Own: British Women Novelists from Brontë to Lessing*, rev. edn, London, 1982, p. 259.
8 Dodd, op. cit., p. 8.
9 ibid., p. 14.
10 P. Wright, *On Living in an Old Country: The National Past in Contemporary Britain*, London, 1985, p. 17.
11 ibid.
12 ibid., pp. 33–42.
13 ibid., p. 36.
14 Hall *et al.*, op. cit., p. 147.
15 M. Girouard, *The Return to Camelot*, New Haven, 1981, p. 62.
16 ibid., p. 14.
17 B. Doyle, 'The Invention of English' in Colls and Dodd, op. cit., p. 93.
18 J. R. Green, *History of the English People*, London, 1877, pp. 8, 9.
19 ibid., p. 9.
20 ibid., p. 13.

21 ibid.
22 Writers who followed Conan Doyle in giving a picture of 'Englishness' include A. E. W. Mason (with *Lawrence Clavering*, 1897), Baroness Orczy (with *The Scarlet Pimpernel*, 1905, and its successors) and Rafael Sabatini, particularly with *The Hounds of God* (1928).
23 A. Howkins, 'The Discovery of Rural England', in Colls and Dodd, op. cit., p. 70.
24 J. A. Froude, *Short Studies in Great Subjects*, London, 1898, cited in Howkins, op. cit., p. 70.
25 Howkins, op. cit., p. 71.
26 ibid., p. 72. Howkins also cites editors of Tudor and Stuart music such as E. H. Fellowes (whose *The English Madrigal School* began publication in 1913), R. R. Terry and J. A. Fuller Maitland. The Dolmetsch reproduction of ancient instruments is also noted as a significant innovation of the early years of the twentieth century (p. 86).
27 Wright, op. cit., p. 81.
28 Howkins, op. cit., p. 63.
29 ibid., p. 69.
30 ibid., p. 63.
31 P. Brooker and P. Widdowson, 'A Literature for England', in Colls and Dodd, op. cit., p. 126.
32 ibid., p. 138.
33 Howkins, op. cit., p. 75.
34 ibid.
35 A. E. W. Mason, *Lawrence Clavering*, London, 1897.
36 Wright, op. cit., p. 85.
37 See, for example, the passage in *The Lion's Skin* (1911), which describes the heroine on her first appearance: 'Mr. Caryll observed – and be it known that he had the very shrewdest eye for a woman, as became one of the race from which on his mother's side he sprang – that she was middling tall, chastely slender, having, as he judged from her high waist, a fine clean length of limb. All this he observed and approved' (p.26).
38 J. Berger, *Ways of Seeing*, New York, 1973, p. 36.

6 Class, the gospel of work and 'hazard'

1 M. Girouard, *The Return to Camelot*, New Haven, 1981, p. 62.
2 P. Wright, *On Living in an Old Country: The National Past in Contemporary Britain*, London, 1985, p. 19.
3 F. Bédarida, *A Social History of England*, tr. A. S. Forster, London, 1979, p. 281.
4 ibid.
5 ibid., p. 282.
6 A. Giddens, *The Class Structure of the Advanced Societies*, London, 1973, p. 166.
7 R. Hewison, 'The Historical Novel: Violent Inventions', *Times Literary Supplement*, 28 August 1981.

7 'Brute heroes' and 'spirited heroines'

1 G. Greer, *The Female Eunuch*, New York, 1971, p. 176.
2 T. Modleski, *Loving with a Vengeance: Mass-Produced Fantasies for Women*, Hamden, Conn., 1982, p. 40.
3 ibid., p. 45.
4 ibid.
5 T. Bennett and J. Woollacott, *Bond and Beyond: The Political Career of a Popular Hero*, London, 1987, pp. 221, 225.
6 J. Radway, *Reading the Romance: Women, Patriarchy and Popular Literature*, Chapel Hill, 1984, pp. 127–8.
7 Modleski, op. cit., p. 31.
8 ibid., pp. 12–15.
9 ibid., p. 15.
10 ibid., p. 36.
11 ibid., p. 44.
12 S. Brownmiller, *Against our Will: Men, Women and Rape*, New York, p. 360.
13 Modleski, op, cit., p. 41.
14 E. Hunter, *The Bride Price*, Toronto, 1974, p. 174, cited in Modleski, op. cit., p. 41.
15 E. Showalter, 'Review Essay: Literary Criticism', *Signs*, 1 (1975), cited in Modleski, op. cit., p. 25.
16 P. Macherey, *A Theory of Literary Production*, tr. G. Wall, London, 1978, pp. 155–6.
17 A. Marwick, *Britain in the Century of Total War: War, Peace and Social Change 1900–1967*, Harmondsworth, 1970, pp. 111 and 193.
18 ibid., pp. 105–6.
19 D. Thomson, *England in the Twentieth Century*, Harmondsworth, 1965, p. 87.
20 ibid.
21 D. Riley, 'The Free Mothers', *History Workshop*, 11 (Spring 1981), pp. 59–120.
22 C. L. Mowatt, *Britain Between the Wars*, London, 1968, p. 214.
23 Thomson, op. cit., p. 87.
24 J. A. Hodge, *The Private World of Georgette Heyer*, London, 1984, p. 7.
25 P. Mann, *The Facts about Romantic Fiction*, London, 1974.
26 ibid., pp. 12, 14.
27 In Stanley Weyman's *Under the Red Robe* (1894), the hero, lapped around with feminine orderliness and care for comfort, concluded that in the 'masculine' world of the gaming houses of Paris he had 'lived like a pig' (p. 77), and when the soldiers from Auch threaten that orderliness, leaving their grimy boots in the dining room, for instance, he is furious and throws them out.
28 J. Russ, 'Somebody is Trying to Kill Me and I Think It's My Husband: The Modern Gothic', *Journal of Popular Culture*, 6 (1973), p. 684, cited in Modleski, op. cit., p. 70.
29 J. Melville, 'Acts of Violence', *New Statesman and Society*, 17 May 1991, p. 24.
30 ibid.

31 L. Mulvey, 'Visual Pleasure and the Narrative Cinema', in T. Bennett, S. Boyd-Bowman, C. Mercer and J. Woollacott (eds), *Popular Television and Film*, London, 1981, cited in Bennett and Woollacott, op. cit., p. 153.
32 Modleski, op. cit., p. 45; Radway, op. cit., p. 127.
33 A. E. W. Mason, *The Courtship of Morrice Buckler*, London, 1901, p. 124.
34 Modleski, op. cit., pp. 52–6.
35 Russ, op. cit., p. 681.
36 Radway, op. cit., p. 128.
37 A. R. Jones, 'Mills & Boon Meets Feminism', in J. Radford (ed.), *The Progress of Romance*, London, 1986, 195–220, p. 203.
38 ibid., p. 210.
39 ibid., p. 215.

8 History, best-sellers and the media

1 See, for example, the ways in which the reader is drawn to take upon him- or herself attitudes towards England which are clearly compensatory described in T. Bennett and J. Woollacott (eds), *Bond and Beyond: The Political Career of a Popular Hero*, London, 1987, p. 107.
2 ibid., p. 225: 'The hero under physical threat inevitably produces a frisson of desire in the heroine . . . in taking care of the wounded hero, heroines frequently take over phallic authority.'
3 In Stanley Weyman's *Abbess of Vlaye* (1904), the heroine, after cutting the hero free from his bonds as they both hurtle, strapped to their horses, across the French countryside in the power of the Crocans, turns faint and has to be helped to a nearby hut by the hero. In the same way the heroine of Barbara Cartland's *Love for Sale* (1980) saves the hero, when they have both been tied up and left to die in a cellar by the villain, by gnawing through his bonds with teeth toughened by her habit of breaking nuts with them; but as soon as they both return safely to the hero's house she faints and has to be carried to her room.
4 A motif in both *Starvecrow Farm* (1905) and *My Lady Rotha* (1927).
5 Bennett and Woollacott, op. cit., p. 227.
6 T. Modleski, *Loving with a Vengeance: Mass-Produced Fantasies for Women*, Hamden, Conn., 1982, p. 45.
7 Bennett and Woollacott, op. cit., p. 104.
8 C. Cockburn, *Bestseller*, London, 1972, p. 95.
9 See, for example, the account of Lady Caroline Lamb's behaviour in *The Young Melbourne* by Lord David Cecil (London, 1939).
10 E.g. in the *Guardian*, Friday, 8 January 1988 (p. 14), the 'Top Hundred Chart of Paperback Bestsellers' shows that, after two thrillers and a book by Jackie Collins, the bestsellers were two sagas, one by Catherine Cookson (*The Moth*) and one by Barbara Taylor Bradford (*Act of Will*), and if English sales alone had been taken into account, they would have been second and fourth on the list. Another saga, *Dark Angel*, by Virginia Andrews followed at number nine. In the previous year Barbara Taylor Bradford's *Hold the Dream* had been 'queen of the sagas

and the year's top seller' (*Guardian*, Monday, 5 January 1987, p. 9), with Catherine Cookson's *Dinner of Herbs* at number five.

11 E. Tincknell, 'Female Fortunes: Women, Power and Consumption in the Popular Saga', an open seminar held at the Centre for Popular Culture, Sheffield City Polytechnic, 14 March 1991.
12 Modleski, op. cit., p. 97.
13 ibid.
14 ibid.
15 Tincknell, seminar cited above.
16 ibid.
17 P. Wright, *On Living in an Old Country: The National Past in Contemporary Britain*, London, 1985, p. 17.
18 S. Bann, *The Clothing of Clio*, Cambridge, 1984, p. 6.
19 *Radio Times*, 8–14 June 1991, p. 92.
20 P. Bourdieu, quoted in J. Donald and C. Mercer, 'Reading and Realism', Unit 15, in *Popular Culture*, Open University Course U203, Milton Keynes, 1981, p. 71.
21 J. Gibbs, letter, 19 June 1991.
22 Modleski, op. cit., p. 36.

Bibliography

Where appropriate, the original date of publication is the first item after the title in parentheses.

PRIMARY SOURCES

Bishop, Sheila, *The Phantom Garden*, London: Hurst & Blackett, 1974.
Cartland, Barbara, *The Bored Bridegroom* (1974), *The Magnificent Marriage* (1974), *The Proud Princess* (1976), all in *The Best of Barbara Cartland*, London: Marshall Cavendish, 1978.
Conan Doyle, Sir Arthur, *Sir Nigel* (1906), in *The Conan Doyle Historical Romances*, vol. I, London: John Murray, 1931.
——*The White Company* (1891), London: John Murray/Jonathan Cape, 1931.
Courtney, Caroline, *Love Unmasked*, London: Arlington Books, 1979.
——*A Wager for Love*, London: Arlington Books, 1979.
Darcy, Clare, *Letty*, London: Macdonald, 1980.
Dean, Dinah, *The Briar Rose*, London: Mills & Boon, 1986.
Dunnett, Dorothy, *The Game of Kings*, London: Cassell, 1962.
Farnol, Jeffrey, *The Broad Highway* (1910), London: Chivers, 1973.
——*The High Adventure* (1925), London: Diploma Press, 1974.
Gibb, Mary Ann, *A Most Romantic City*, London: Hurst & Blackett, 1976.
Heyer, Georgette, *The Black Moth* (1921), London: Pan in association with Heinemann, 1965.
——*A Civil Contract*, London: Heinemann, 1961.
——*The Quiet Gentleman*, London: Heinemann, 1951.
——*Regency Buck* (1935), London: Pan in association with Heinemann, 1959.
——*These Old Shades*, London: Heinemann, 1926.
Lang, Frances, *The Filigree Bird*, London: Robert Hale, 1981.
Macdonald, Eva, *Cromwell's Spy*, London: Robert Hale, 1976.
——*House of Secrets*, London: Robert Hale, 1980.
Mason, Alfred E. W., *Clementina* (1901), Birmingham: C. Combridge, 1976.
——*The Courtship of Morrice Buckler* (1896), London: Macmillan, 1901.

——*Lawrence Clavering*, London: Hodder & Stoughton, 1897.

Oliver, Marina, *Highwayman's Hazard*, London: Robert Hale, 1983.

Orczy, Emmuska (Baroness) *The Adventures of the Scarlet Pimpernel* (1929), London: Hutchinson, 1974.

——*The Scarlet Pimpernel* (1905), London: Brockhampton Press, 1961.

——*The Triumph of the Scarlet Pimpernel* (1922), Bath: Lythway reprint, 1969.

Sabatini, Rafael, *The Hounds of God* (1928), London: Hutchinson, 1974.

——*The Marquis of Carabas*, London: Hutchinson, 1940.

——*Scaramouche* (1921), London: Hutchinson, 1927.

——*The Strolling Saint*, London: Stanley Paul & Co., 1913.

——*The Trampling of the Lilies* (1906), London: Hutchinson, 1927.

Stables, Mira, *Golden Barrier*, London: Robert Hale, 1981.

——*Quality Maid*, London: Robert Hale, 1973.

Tenet, Rowena, *Bewitching Imposter*, London: Robert Hale, 1983.

Weyman, Stanley, *The Abbess of Vlaye* (1904), London: Dent, n. d.

——*The Castle Inn* (1898), London: Wayfarers' Library, n. d.

——*Count Hannibal*, London: Smith Elder, 1901.

——*A Gentleman of France*, London: Longmans, 1895.

——*My Lady Rotha*, London: Ward Lock, 1927.

——*Starvecrow Farm* (1905), London: Wayfarers' Library, n. d.

——*Under the Red Robe* (1894), London: Methuen, 1940.

CRITICAL AND HISTORICAL TEXTS

Altick, Richard, *The English Common Reader*, Chicago: University of Chicago Press, 1957.

Arnold, Matthew, *Culture and Anarchy* in *Selected Essays*, ed. Noel Annan, Oxford: Oxford University Press, 1964.

Ashworth, William, *An Economic History of England 1870–1939*, London: Methuen, 1960.

Bann, Stephen, *The Clothing of Clio*, Cambridge: Cambridge University Press, 1984.

Barthes, Roland, *Mythologies*, tr. A. Lavers, London: Jonathan Cape, 1972.

——'The Reality Effect', in *French Literary Theory Today*, ed. Tzetvan Todorov, tr. R. Carter, Cambridge: Cambridge University Press, 1982.

——*S/Z*, tr. R. Miller, London: Jonathan Cape, 1975.

Bédarida, François, *A Social History of England*, tr. A. S. Forster, London: Methuen, 1979.

Beer, Gillian, *Romance*, London: Methuen, 1970.

Bennett, Tony and Janet Woollacott (eds), *Bond and Beyond: The Political Career of a Popular Hero*, London: Macmillan, 1987.

Berger, John *Ways of Seeing*, New York: Viking Press, 1973.

Bromley, Roger, *Lost Narratives*, London: Routledge, 1988.

Brownmiller, Susan, *Against Our Will: Men, Women and Rape*, London: Bantam Books, 1976.

Cecil, Lord David, *The Young Melbourne*, London: Constable, 1939.

Chapman, Raymond, *The Sense of the Past in Victorian Literature*, London: Croom Helm, 1986.

Cockburn, Claud, *Bestseller*, London: Sidgwick & Jackson, 1972.

Colls, Robert and Philip Dodd (eds), *Englishness: Politics and Culture 1880–1920,* London: Croom Helm, 1986.

Eco, Umberto, *Travels in Hyper-reality*, tr. W. Weaver, London: Picador, 1987 (first pub. 1986 as *Faith in Fakes*).

Fleishman, Avrom, *The English Historical Novel: Walter Scott to Virginia Woolf*, Baltimore: Johns Hopkins Press, 1971.

Girouard, Marc, *The Return to Camelot*, New Haven: Yale University Press, 1981.

Green, John R., *History of the English People,* London: Macmillan, 1877.

Greer, Germaine, *The Female Eunuch*, New York: McGraw Hill, 1971.

Hall, Stuart, C. Critcher, T. Jefferson, J. Clarke and B. Roberts, *Policing the Crisis: Mugging, The State and Law and Order,* Basingstoke: Macmillan, 1978.

Henderson, Harry B. III, *Versions of the Past*, Oxford: Oxford University Press, 1974.

Hobsbaum, Eric J., *Industry and Empire*, Penguin, 1968.

Hodge, Jane Aiken, *The Private World of Georgette Heyer*, London: Bodley Head, 1984.

Iser, Wolfgang, *The Implied Reader: Patterns in Communication in Prose Fiction from Bunyan to Becket*, Baltimore: Johns Hopkins University Press, 1974.

Jones, Ann Rosalind, 'Mills & Boon Meets Feminism', in Jean Radford (ed.), *The Progress of Romance*, London: Routledge, 1986.

Langan, Mary and Bill Schwarz (eds), *Crises in the British State 1880–1930*, London: Hutchinson, 1985.

Leavis, Queenie D., *Fiction and the Reading Public* (1932), London: Chatto & Windus, 1965.

Lukács, Georg, *The Historical Novel*, tr. H. and S. Mitchell, Harmondsworth: Penguin, 1969.

Macherey, Pierre, *A Theory of Literary Production*, tr. G. Wall, London: Routledge & Kegan Paul, 1978.

Martin, Graham, 'Readers, Viewers and Texts', in *Popular Culture*, Open University Course U203, Milton Keynes: Open University Press, 1981.

Marwick, Arthur, *Britain in the Century of Total War: War, Peace and Social Change 1900–1967*, Harmondsworth: Penguin, 1970.

Modleski, Tania, *Loving with a Vengeance: Mass-Produced Fantasies for Women*, Hamden: Archon Books, 1982.

Mowatt, Charles L., *Britain Between the Wars 1918–1940*, London: Methuen, 1955.

Pawling, Christopher, *Popular Fiction and Social Change*, London: Macmillan, 1984.

Propp, Valdimir, *The Morphology of the Folktale* (1928), Austin, Texas: Texas University Press, 1968.

Radford, Jean (ed.) *The Progress of Romance*, London: Routledge, 1986.

Radway, Janice, *Reading the Romance: Women, Patriarchy and Popular Literature*, Chapel Hill/University of North Carolina Press, 1984.

Rance, Nicholas, *The Historical Novel and Popular Politics*, London: Vision Press, 1975.

Selden, Raman, *A Reader's Guide to Contemporary Literary Theory*, Brighton: Harvester, 1985.

Showalter, Elaine, *A Literature of their Own*, Princeton: Princeton University Press, 1977.

Swingewood, Alan, *The Myth of Mass Culture* (1970), London: Macmillan, 1977.

Thomson, David, *England in the Nineteenth Century, 1815–1914*, Harmondsworth: Penguin, 1950.

——*England in the Twentieth Century*, Harmondsworth: Penguin, 1965.

Weiner, Martin J., *English Culture and the Decline of the Industrial Spirit 1850–1980*, Cambridge: Cambridge University Press, 1981.

Williams, Raymond, *The Long Revolution*, Harmondsworth: Penguin, 1961.

Williamson, Margaret, 'The Greek Romance', in J. Radford (ed.), *The Progress of Romance*, London: Routledge, 1986.

Wright, Patrick, *On Living in an Old Country: The National Past in Contemporary Britain*, London: Verso, 1985.

PERIODICAL ARTICLES

Avery, Gillian, 'The Very Pink of Propriety', *The Times Literary Supplement*, 21 September 1984, 1064.

Black, J. and Pearson, D., 'Selling Historical Fiction', *Bookseller*, 28 September 1985, 1330–1.

Hewison, R., 'The Historical Novel: Violent Inventions', *Times Literary Supplement*, 28 August 1981, 991.

Langham, J., 'The Changing Face of Romance', Mills & Boon Press Release, October 1986.

Mann, Peter H., 'Romantic Fiction and its Readers', *Poetics*, 14, nos. 1/2, April 1985.

——'The Facts about Romantic Fiction', Mills & Boon, 1974.

Melville, Joy, 'Acts of Violence', *New Statesman and New Society*, 17 May 1991, 24.

Riley, Denise, 'The Free Mothers', *History Workshop*, 11, Spring 1981, 59–120.

Index